# Man's Destiny in the Books of Wisdom

alba house. DIVISION OF THE SOCIETY OF ST. PAUL
STATEN ISLAND, N.Y. 10314

# Man's Destiny in the Books of Wisdom

Evode Beaucamp, O.F.M.

Original title: La Sagesse et le Destin des Élus, published by Éditions Fleurus, Paris.
Translated by John Clarke, O.C.D.

Nihil Obstat:
  Donald A. Panella, S.T.L., S.S.L.
  Censor Librorum
Imprimatur:
  Joseph O'Brien, S.T.D., V.G.
  Archdiocese of New York
  March 16, 1970

Library of Congress Catalog Card Number: 73:110596
SBN: 8189-0159-4

Designed, printed and bound in the U.S.A. by the Pauline Fathers and Brothers of the Society of St. Paul, 2187 Victory Blvd., Staten Island, N.Y. 10314 as part of their communications apostolate.

# CONTENTS

Introduction                                                    vii

## The Book of Proverbs                                          1

A. From Solomon's court to entry into the kingdom                1

B. Portrait of the wise man                                     12

C. The fruits of wisdom                                         20

D. Wisdom, door of the covenant                                 27

E. Eve and Mary                                                 32

F. Wisdom and the created universe                              40

## The Book of Job                                              45

A. The suffering of a child of Israel                           46

B. God's silence                                                54

C. The hand of God                                              62

D. The judgment of God on the world                            67

E. Yahweh makes his appearance                                  73

F. The impenetrable mystery of wisdom                           80

The Book of Ecclesiastes                                        85

    A. In pursuit of the wind                               85

    B. Value of the present moment                          92

    C. Wisdom is beyond the reach of man                    97

The Book of Ecclesiasticus (or the Wisdom of Jesus the
    son of Sirach)                                        103

    A. Israel becomes conscious of itself                  103

    B. The privilege of wisdom and the search for human unity   116

    C. Ben Sirach's optimism                               124

The Book of Daniel                                             135

    A. The trial of fidelity                               136

    B. The people of saints and the world                 148

    C. Wisdom reveals the mystery of the end of time       156

The Book of Wisdom                                             167

    A. The just one despised by the world                 168

    B. The privilege of wisdom                             179

    C. The universe is invited to conversion              191

Conclusion: The Old Testament and the development of
    the spiritual life                                     205

# UNDER THE HAND OF GOD

Each member of the community in the New Israel will have to become involved and assume responsibility for his own actions. He will be rewarded for his fidelity or punished for his sins. The Chosen People will no longer be the holy people but the people of saints. Thus had the exilic prophets announced: Jeremiah, Ezekiel, and Second Isaiah.

What must now be formed is not the conscience of Israel but that of the Israelite. The prophets will give place to the sages whose writings will take on a growing importance in the post-exilic literature. Wisdom will transmit the message of the God of Sinai to anyone willing to listen.

The wisdom books which will now nourish our meditation, viz., Proverbs, Job, Ecclesiastes (or Qoheleth), Ecclesiasticus (or Ben Sirach), Daniel, and Wisdom, were very much enjoyed at one time. The first Christian generations drew teachings from the least detail of Scripture and enriched their spiritual life thereby. The writings of the sages offered them an inexhaustible mine of deep and edifying reflections. Both the liturgy and the breviary give these writings a place of honor in their readings and responses.

These readings enjoy less favor today. The reason for this is that the modern reader expresses demands scarcely thought of by his predecessors. First, he does not agree with texts taken violently out of context and frequently given an interpretation to bring them into harmony with an entirely different thought. The modern reader needs comprehensive perspectives and syntheses as well as exactitude. Secondly, should he really undertake the reading of the wisdom writings? He feels ill at ease in their long developments, losing the thread of thought and often misunderstanding the real meaning of the words used. He has just familiarized himself with the reading of the prophets, and now he must go in search of a *key* which will open up to him the writings of the sages.

Is he to find this key in a comparison of the inspired books with similar writings in Egypt, in Babylon, in Greece, or in Canaan? There exists no literary genre in our sacred books which does not have an equivalent or a model in these other literatures, whether it be a question of collections of opinions, dialogues on suffering, or reflections on life's purpose. Such a *comparison,* though very interesting, is not sufficient for explaining the spiritual meaning of the sacred text.

Will this key be supplied by *modern exegesis?* Modern exegesis can guide us through the maze of Israel's wisdom books. The reader will discover in this exegesis a sustained effort to solve one *central problem*: the *retribution of human actions.*

From the beginning Israel's fidelity to the Covenant will appear as sanctioned by promises of life and threats of death. Up to the Exile, the destiny of individuals, eclipsed by that of the nation, is not taken into account. It is only after Jeremiah's message that these same sanctions are applied to the individual, for now the New Covenant will demand personal responsibility. Wisdom enters upon the scene inviting men to eat at her table. She too promises and threatens; she encourages and warns. She makes it clear that the good will be rewarded and the evil punished in this world.

This doctrine of temporal retribution, however, when applied to individuals, will soon bristle with difficulties. Does it not lead one to believe that prosperity is the touchstone of virtue and

misfortune that of sin? Jewish society, while understanding the
instructive value of suffering, will come to look upon the unfortunate man as one rejected. There will be no lack of good
apostles counselling him to humble repentance. The strong
protest of the Book of Job will rise up against this odious
judgment cast upon a neighbor's suffering. Its author, while not
solving the problem, will deny that misfortune is a sign of vice
and good fortune a sign of virtue. Ecclesiastes, less sanguine but
just as categorical, will uphold Job in its conclusions: in this
world we vainly seek for the reward of the good and the punishment of the wicked.

Faced with such strong statements, Jewish thought is forced
to renounce the idea of divine justice or to seek out its effects in
a *great beyond.* And it is evidently in this latter direction that
Israel's Wisdom points. In the second quarter of the second
century, during the persecution by Antiochus Epiphanes, the
apocalypses and especially the Book of Daniel will open up the
perspective of a *general resurrection of bodies.* A century later,
an Alexandrian writer, in Wisdom, will enrich biblical theology
with the precious Greek notion of the *immortality of the soul.*

Our purpose is not to contest the interest of this teaching. We
shall confine ourselves to emphasizing that it does not include
the total content of our inspired books. If everything were to be
reduced to this metaphysical skeleton, these books would offer
only an historical interest. The Christian soul, accustomed to
meditating upon the last ends of man from the dawn of its
consciousness, would draw meager profit from them.

Moreover, the effort at reflection on the part of the sages is
found buried in a multitude of considerations which are only
loosely connected to the problem of retribution.

We are curious about this Wisdom who stands out so prom-
inently. She holds such a position of importance that she cannot
be relegated to the background. It is she, rather than the purely
rational considerations, who merits to attract our attention.

Everything becomes clear, we think, when we discover a

certain connection between Wisdom and the New Covenant preached by Jeremiah. We see this same Wisdom, after having taught the kings, has taken upon herself the formation of the individual in the bosom of the royal nation the New Israel is to be. It is Wisdom who welcomes the Elect of God, who directs their journey, and who specifies the direction of their destiny.

This link between Wisdom and the Covenant is not always evident, especially in the first wisdom books. Proverbs, Job, and Ecclesiastes deal with matters which seem foreign to the Election, matters which Israel shares with other civilizations.

Let us be on our guard in believing this, for we would be reasoning as though the fact of the Sinai Covenant were grafted upon the universal concept of a just and rewarding God. Human reasoning would be satisfied with such a postulate, but reality plays tricks with our way of reasoning. In reality, the Covenant is the first idea Israel received; and it is in this singular experience Israel will reflect on God and his perfections, on man and the value of his actions. If there is to be any question of retribution, it is not a question of the retribution of man but the retribution of the Elect. The memory of the Covenant, even when it is explicitly evoked, underlies every page of the Old Testament.

Some will object: the Wisdom of Proverbs is directed towards humanity in general. Should we not see here a proof that, from the beginning, Wisdom was forced to break asunder the narrow framework of Jewish nationalism?

We must not be taken in by words. Wisdom made no universal appeal either from the beginning or for a long time afterwards. She was satisfied with making disciples in Israel. She had not become conscious of other civilizations, nor thought of defining her position with regard to them; everything took place as though she were alone in the world. When Hellenism brings pressure upon Jewish society, Israel will be forced to claim her irreducible originality. Ben Sirach will point out the relationship between Wisdom and the Law of Sinai, the relationship between the tradition of the fathers with the history of Salvation. A few years later, the Book of Daniel will set this same Wisdom in opposition to the wisdom of the Chaldeans in order to accentuate her superiority. An Alexandrian Jew, finally, will present her as Wisdom par excellence. She alone is capable of guiding men. Thus it will be only at the end of this evolution that she will be invested with a universal mission. And even then we cannot say of Wisdom she has ceased to be associated with the idea of the Covenant.

We must still point out the role played by Wisdom with reference to the Covenant.

Too often we are tempted to look upon the sages as the upholders of ancient traditions just as we look upon the prophets as the foretellers of the future. Although it is true the latter opened up new horizons to Israel and the former transmitted the experience of the past, it is the sages rather than the prophets who will be assigned the duty of forging the future.

Before the great tribulation, the prophets, Yahweh's immediate heralds, reminded Israel of the Covenant's demands which were still in force though greatly compromised. New prophets foretold another Covenant which was to be more intimate and beautiful; but when the voice of the last of these prophets died out this New Covenant was still only a promise. Between the Covenant which is now only a memory and the one which is only a hope there will be a period of transition in which hearts will have to prepare themselves and a renewed community will have to undertake the task of prefiguring the future kingdom. It will be the work of Wisdom to aid them in this task by revealing to them the difficulties and the grandeurs of their destiny as the Elect.

The wisdom books took form and came to life under these circumstances. We discover in them the developing of a drama which announces and prepares for ours. Through Wisdom God calls his children, inviting them to surrender the care of their destiny to him (Proverbs). Hardly have they set out on the road when they strike against an apparently invincible obstacle (Job). Now life seems to be confined within the narrow limits of the present moment (Ecclesiastes). The adventure cannot be thus confined, for it has a deep meaning. Failing to penetrate its meaning, the understanding will be aided by faith; and the Elect will intone his hymn of thanksgiving (Ben Sirach). And behold a radiant dawn points to the horizon: everything will come to an end beyond earthly frontiers (Daniel). But already the Elect, upon whom the Hand of God has been placed, possesses in the depths of his soul the guarantees of eternity which assure him victory over death (Wisdom).

There remains only the conclusion of the drama: the establishment of this New Covenant and this New Israel in which each one will know the laws of his involvement and will receive the first fruits of his eternal destiny. Hearts are ready, for Christ is about to appear.

# Man's Destiny in the Books of Wisdom

# THE BOOK OF PROVERBS

1 The Book of Proverbs is composed of a prologue (chapters 1-9), several collections of maxims (10-31), and an appendix (31).

The *collections of maxims or proverbs,* making up the most important part of the work, are of different dates and origins. The two principal ones, attributed to Solomon and to the friends of Hezekiah, gather proverbs customary among the sages of the royal administration at Jerusalem.

An identical author could have written the *prologue* and the *appendix* later. Short sentences give way to wider developments and warm exhortations, the style of which reminds one of the sermons found in the deuteronomic code. Although it is difficult to be exact about the date, it seems we should set their redaction at the end of the Exile or even in the first years after the Return.

A.- FROM SOLOMON'S COURT TO ENTRY INTO THE KINGDOM

There is scarcely any country whose literature has not been enriched by the common sense of its people. However, it is not the voice of the common people in ancient Egypt's towns and cities that one hears in the maxims and other wisdom writings. Rather it is the voices of the Pharaohs and their court; they speak, and they speak for themselves.

An old king of the sixth dynasty transmits the "best of his

inner self" to Nerikara his son. Amenemhet, founder of the twelfth dynasty, teaches Sesostris, his successor, not to give equal trust to his friends and confidants; he puts him on guard against man's ingratitude which he will one day experience.

We have, then, the wisdom of kings and of ministers, reminding us of how the God of Israel favored Joseph, son of Jacob. There are the maxims of Ptah Hotep, whose magnificent mortuary chapel may be seen at Saqqarah, necropolis of Memphis. He instructs his son according to *"the ancient sayings in order that he might be admired by the great."*

There was the wisdom of the scribes taught to their numerous functionaries who made up the pride and strength of the Pharaoh state. We should keep in mind that writing remained the monopoly of this privileged class who were taught from childhood by stern masters to copy the teachings of the ancients. As trained courtiers and government officials these Egyptian scribes were proud of their education. Though it cost them many a sacrifice, it raised them above the miserable lot of the common people. This gave rise to the famous *"Satire on trades"* by Douaouf, which he composed for his son. The brilliant career of the scribes is here compared with the rough work of the laborer.

✿   ✿   ✿

The greater part of biblical Proverbs was undoubtedly inspired by this *aristocratic wisdom* of the Nile Valley. Like its models, Proverbs bears witness to an evident solicitude for the princes and the people of the court who from Solomon to Hezekiah were dedicated to weilding and influence on the social and political evolution of the country.

However, we find in Proverbs something entirely different from a simple adaptation of Egyptian maxims. We find here the spirit of the Sinai Covenant which gives these writings a new sound and meaning.

Before all else, Proverbs gives testimony of the desire to maintain *justice* in the kingdom. Much more than at Thebes at the time of the socialist Pharaohs of the Middle Empire, it is upon justice that the throne at Jerusalem is to be built (16, 12; 25, 5; 29, 14); also, the function par excellence of the *king* is to mete out justice to each one. From the beginning of his revolt against his father David, Absalom cries out at the city's gates: "Oh that I were judge in the land! Then every man with a suit or cause might come to me, and I would give him justice" (2 Sam. 15, 4).

We are well aware of Solomon's famous judgment in which his wisdom was manifested to all the people, that wisdom which he had begged from the Lord on the day of his accession to the throne: "And all Israel heard of the judgment which the king had rendered; and they stood in awe of the king, because they perceived that the wisdom of God was in him, to render justice" (1 Kgs. 3, 28).

Proverbs points out how the king restores and upholds order in the city through his vigilance: "A king who sits on the throne of judgment winnows all evil with his eyes" (20, 8). The happiness of all depends upon his good will: "In the light of the king's face there is life, and his favor is like the clouds that bring the spring rain" (16, 15).

The king must not fall under anyone's control, vested as he is with superhuman prestige: "As the heavens for the height and the earth for depth, so the mind of the kings is unsearchable" (25, 3).

His sentence must be received as an infallible decision: "Inspired decisions are on the lips of the king; his mouth does not sin in judgment" (16, 10).

The reason for this is that the king is God's authentic representative, whose throne has *"righteousness and justice"* as its foundation (Ps. 97, 2). God enlightens and guides him in judgment: "The king's heart is a stream of water in the hand of the Lord; he turns it wherever he will" (21, 1).

The kings learned much from Wisdom. The princes of Israel were not free from sin as history attests. From Nathan to Jeremiah the prophets were constantly correcting kings. The sages will follow suit, but they will correct with more reserve. While maintaining a certain moderation, however, they will always point out the road to duty. The portrait of an ideal king drawn by a clever courtier will serve as a lesson. For example, the poet who composed the wedding hymn for Ahaz makes several valuable reflections, and the future was to show how opportune and effective these were. Counsel was cleverly given under the cloak of flattery: "You love righteousness and hate wickedness" (Ps. 45, 7).

Proverbs traces out the line of conduct befitting kings: "A wise king winnows the wicked, and drives the wheel over them" (20, 26). "It is the glory of God to conceal things, but the glory of kings to search things out" (25, 2). "If a king judges the poor with equity his throne will be established for ever" (29, 14).

The sages condemn those kings who fail in their duty: "It is an abomination to kings to do evil, for the throne is established by righteousness" (16, 12).

The king's infidelity will give rise to sufferings for others: "When the righteous are in authority, the people rejoice; but when wicked rule, the people groan" (29, 2). Though these lessons remain somewhat cautious and veiled regarding David's successors, Wisdom speaks more openly regarding the court's functionaries. She guides the young who have made this their career. They are not to use their office for gain: "The hand of the diligent will rule, while the slothful will be put to forced labor" (12, 24). Let them be neither presumptuous nor insolent: "Do not put yourself forward in the king's presence or stand in the place of the great; for it is better to be told, 'come up here,' than to be put lower in the presence of the prince" (25, 6-7). Wisdom, as the wisdom of Egypt, wants to form accomplished servants by showing them how to gain or lose the king's favor: "Righteous lips are the delight of the king, and he loves him who speaks what is right" (16, 13). "He who loves purity of heart and whose speech is gracious, will have the king as his friend" (22, 11). "A servant who deals wisely has the king's favor, but his wrath falls on one who acts shamefully" (14, 35).

In the first ranks of these privileged men are the *"counselors"* in whose presence the king *"weighs his plans"* (20, 18). These men made up, along with the priests and "professional" prophets, one of the most essential elements in the royal administration. Do not Jeremiah's detractors counter his threats with traditional assurances? "Come, let us make plots against Jeremiah, for the law shall not perish from the priest, nor counsel from the wise, nor the word from the prophet" (Jer. 18, 18).

Proverbs underscores the importance of counselors in the State government: "Where there is no guidance, a people falls; but in an abundance of counselors there is safety" (11, 14; cf. 24, 6).

It is because of failure to follow their advice that kings fall: thus Absalom, for not having listened to the wise Ahitophel, ruined in a few days the advantages he had acquired in his rebellion against his father (2 Sam. 16, 15-17, 23); and Rehoboam, because of his obstinacy which was stronger than the experience of old men, brought about the secession of the ten tribes of the North (1 Kgs. 12, 6,19).

At the side of the counselors stood the *messengers* whose role in public affairs was very important. Kings chose them carefully and demanded of them elementary qualities: intelligence, zeal, and fidelity: "He who sends a message by the hand of a fool cuts off his own feet and drinks violence" (26, 6). "Like vinegar to his teeth, and smoke to his eyes, so is the sluggard to those

who send him" (10, 26). "Like the cold of snow in the time of
harvest is the faithful messenger to those who send him, he re-
freshes the spirit of his masters" (25, 13).

Furthermore, this choice required of the messenger a conformity with the nature of the message: the man being identified,
so to speak, with the mission entrusted to him. We recall David's
spontaneous cry. While impatiently awaiting the outcome of the
battle between Joab and the rebellious Absalom, the lookout man
identifies the messenger as Ahimaaz, son of Sodac: "He is a good
man, and comes with good tidings" exclaims the king (2 Sam.
18, 27). A good messenger is a sign of good news.

Proverbs states: "An evil man seeks only rebellion and, a
cruel messenger will be sent against him" (17, 11).

Finally, there is a class of functionaries whose moral value
to the State is of extreme importance, viz., the *judges*. They hold
the king's judiciary power through delegation. Proverbs reminds them, as had Moses and the prophets, that their primary
duty is one of impartiality. It was the iniquity of Israel's judges,
among other causes, that brought down the chastisement it
received.

Their venality is to be severely condemned: "A wicked man
accepts a bribe from the bosom to pervert the ways of
justice" (17, 23).

Proverbs reminds judges that desire for gain does not pay:
"He who is greedy for the unjust gain makes trouble for his
household, but he who hates bribes will live" (15, 27).

Before all else, their chief crime is the violation of justice;
and through this violation they offend a just God: "He who
justifies the wicked and he who condemns the righteous are
both alike an abomination to the Lord" (17, 15). "It is not
good to be partial to a wicked man, or to deprive a righteous
man of justice" (18, 5).

Rare are those who treat the poor justly and without partiality: "Partiality in judging is not good. He who says to the wicked,
'You are innocent,' will be cursed by peoples, and abhorred by

nations" (24, 23-24). "To show partiality is not good; but for a piece of bread a man will do wrong" (28, 21). "A righteous man knows the rights of the poor; a wicked man does not understand such knowledge" (29, 7).

\* \* \*

All this is an echo of the wisdom of Egyptian Pharaohs, but it contains a specifically Mosaic note which enriches it. We should add that the Sinai Covenant, with its social demands, could not fail to impress a democratic character upon the State founded by David. This was totally unknown in the Nile Valley. In Israel, the entire nation expands and develops on justice and is dishonored by sin: "Righteousness exalts a nation, but sin is a reproach to any people" (14, 34).

Israel's Wisdom does not disdain addressing herself to little people, such as laborers, merchants, and peasants. To all she prescribes honesty in their transactions: "A false balance is an abomination to the Lord" (11, 1). "A just balance and scales are the Lord's; all the weights in the bag are his work" (16, 11; cf. 20, 10, 23). When rendering witness to the audience: "He who speaks the truth gives honest evidence, but a false witness utters deceit" (12, 17; cf. 14, 5, 25). "A false witness will not go unpunished" (19, 5; cf. 19, 9; 21, 28). "Be not a witness against your neighbor without cause" (24, 28).

An even more remarkable truth is that Proverbs shows an interest especially in work, even farming: "A son who gathers in summer is prudent, but a son who sleeps in harvest brings shame" (10, 5).

Proverbs expresses in a very picturesque way the disastrous effects of negligence: "I passed by the field of a sluggard, by the vineyard of a man without sense; and lo, it was all overgrown with thorns; the ground was covered with nettles, and its stone wall was broken down" (24, 30-31).

Perfectly acquainted with farm life, Proverbs insists the

farmer take care of his livestock, his true riches. If he knows how to do this, he will be supplied with many essentials: "Know well the condition of your flocks, and give attention to your herds; for riches do not last for ever; and does a crown endure to all generations? When the grass is gone and the new growth appears, and the herbage of the mountains is gathered, the lambs will provide your clothing, and the goats the price of a field; and there will be enough goats' milk for your food, for the food of your household and the maintenance of your maidens" (27, 23-27).

Israel's Wisdom takes into account, then, the little people in the villages and country towns, even though the essence of her message is directed to the king and his counselors, messengers, and judges who share in his government.

✿   ✿   ✿

All these great ones of the earth will be swept away like straw by the cyclone of 587. It will swoop down upon the nation because of its sins. During the Exile a displaced Israel will face the future with great expectation. It will meditate upon the New Covenant spoken of by Jeremiah. This covenant will be formed in the hearts of individuals, and the nation will no longer be judged by the conduct of its chiefs. Each will be responsible for his own sins. In the New Israel described by Ezekiel, the successor of David will no longer play an outstanding role. Second Isaiah refers only indirectly to the king. Henceforth it is the whole community of Israel that will inherit royal privileges: "Incline your ear, and come to me; hear, that your soul may live; and I will make with you an everlasting covenant, my steadfast, sure love for David" (Is. 55, 3).

The old Wisdom of Solomon's court will not lose her authority. The exiles are to detach themselves from the errors of the past, not from her riches. Besides the historical books, the laws, the liturgical prayers, they will have to take care not to forget these Proverbs which under the past regime had formed so many men of government and would undoubtedly guide in a useful way the generations to come. This Wisdom who said of herself: "By me kings reign, and rulers decree what is just; by me princes rule, and nobles govern the earth" (8, 15-16), was able to enrich *each child of the new Israel* through her experience: "To you, O men, I call, and my cry is to the sons of men" (8, 4).

After having assured the well-being of yesterday's courtiers, Wisdom will be beneficial to anyone who aspires to be a citizen of tomorrow's kingdom: "Therefore every scribe who has been trained for the kingdom of heaven is like a householder who brings out of his treasure what is new and what is old" (Mt. 13, 52).

Those about to become personally involved in the New Covenant must show qualities recently demanded of those who were directing the whole nation. They will receive an education which until now was reserved for the youth of the Court acquainted with the hardships of the training required of a scribe. This is because Wisdom does not come naturally to man: "Folly is bound up in the heart of a man, but the rod of discipline drives it far from him" (22, 15).

The experience of the ancients is learned with difficulty. One cannot advance along life's path without submitting to *discipline*, nor without accepting the severe correction of reprimands: "He who keeps the commandments keeps his life; he who despises the word will die" (19, 16). "He who heeds instruction is on the path to life; but he who rejects reproof goes astray" (10, 17; cf. 15, 32; 13, 18). "There is severe discipline for him who forsakes the way" (15, 10). "He who is often reproved, yet stiffens his neck will suddenly be broken beyond healing" (29, 1).

Frequently one becomes wise only through the teacher who corrects, the friend who acts rudely, and the father who is severe. True love cannot remain silent when one is going astray: "Better is open rebuke than hidden love" (27, 5). "Faithful are the wounds of a friend; profuse are the kisses of an enemy"

(27, 6). "He who spares the rod hates his son, but he who loves him is diligent to discipline him" (13, 24).

Correction, however, must never be administered blindly: "Discipline your son while there is hope; do not set your heart on his destruction" (19, 18).

Punishment is meaningful only insofar as it is "medicinal," for wisdom is not best inculcated through force; corporal punishment must be administered when persuasion fails: "A rebuke goes deeper into a man of understanding than a hundred blows into a fool" (17, 10).

The disciple must be both receptive and of good will: "How long, O simple ones, will you love being simple? How long will scoffers delight in their scoffing and fools hate knowledge" (1, 22).

Severity is imposed upon rebellious skepticism and its easy ironies: "Condemnation is ready for scoffers, and flogging for the backs of fools" (19, 29). "Strike the scoffer, and the simple will learn prudence" (19, 25; cf. 21, 11). "Drive out the scoffer, and strife will go out, and quarreling and abuse will cease" (22, 10).

For it is a scourge for the city: "Scoffers set a city aflame" (29, 8).

He who refuses to be led docilely will never learn wisdom; pride is impervious to all teaching and ends in ruin: "Pride goes before destruction, and a haughty spirit before a fall" (16, 18). On the contrary, "humility goes before honor" (15, 33; cf. 29, 23).

One should not be overconfident in his own judgment but seek the counsel of the experienced: "There is a way which seems right to a man, but its end is the way to death" (14, 12; cf. 16, 25). "The purpose in a man's mind is like deep water, but a man of understanding will draw it out" (20, 5).

All these are undoubtedly very precise principles of education, but they show that Israel's Wisdom was far in advance of her time. Though Proverbs expressed them without too much insistence, it is firm in pointing out the end in view: "Train up a child in the way he should go, and when he is old he will not depart from it" (22, 6).

Besides the prescriptions on moral practice, Proverbs did not fail to advise the seeker after wisdom to listen to the Teacher of teachers: "Those who seek the Lord understand justice completely" (28, 5).

To remain faithful to the divine commands is the most constant teaching of the Bible. Does not *"fear of the Lord"* mean this; what is it otherwise than losing him, and feeling oneself no longer under the almighty and saving hand of God? This is the reason Proverbs says of this fear that it is: *"a place of security"* (14, 26), *"the source of life"* (14, 27), and *"the school of wisdom"* (15, 33). And one has only to abandon oneself to its infallible direction: "Trust in the Lord with all your heart, and do not rely on your own insight. In all your ways acknowledge him, and he will make straight your paths. Be not wise in your own eyes; fear the Lord, and turn away from evil. My son, do not despise the Lord's discipline or be weary of his reproof, for the Lord reproves him whom he loves, as a father the son in whom he delights" (3, 5-7, 11-12).

\* \* \*

We have only to remind ourselves of the Parables which present stewards and other servants of the royal household to be convinced quickly the Gospel does not despise the old Wisdom of Solomon any more than does post-exilic Judaism. Indeed, it is through the study of the Book of Proverbs that the primitive Church began the formation of her neophytes. It seemed necessary to know how to carry out one's role in the administration of an earthly kingdom in order to enter the kingdom of Heaven. Each kingdom requires the same qualities of understanding: prudence and energy. Christ's Church cannot be a rabble of incapable and blundering people.

To enter more deeply into the matter, we should point out that Christianity did not rise up suddenly as a revelation of God in the bosom of a maladjusted world. Such a shock would have crushed man and discouraged his efforts at making a proper response to the divine call. The gospel message would have initiated a dialogue impossible to be carried on for want of adequate preparation on the part of the human being.

Ordinarily we consider the centuries separating Christ from Adam as the necessary delay in the religious and moral formation of humanity; and this idea is correct. But this too is the time of maturation for man's mind and heart, for the possibilities of his personal commitment. And this is so true that, even today, in the presence of "depersonalized" societies — whether it be a question of those which have only imperfectly made the transition from the nomadic to the settled state or those in which "proletarization" has brought on a kind of uprooting — we can believe the difficulty of adaptation explains why these societies appear to be so much opposed to the preaching of the gospel of the Kingdom of God.

Finally, let us say that in our own day too many Christians attribute only an historic interest in the Book of Proverbs. They have the impression that it will teach them nothing. It is true the Christian does not discover the goal of his journey in the school of Israel's old Wisdom, but he will at least learn that he has not gone off the road. Before giving himself up to lofty speculations on the divine mysteries and even, from time to time, when he has begun to make these mysteries the object of his meditations, would it be useless for him to examine what type of man he really is?

B.- PORTRAIT OF THE WISE MAN

Solomon's Wisdom in no way took upon herself the mission of teaching the Covenant's requirements. It was the duty of the priests as guardians of the Law of Moses to point out the obligations of the faithful. The community was reminded of this on the feasts of Yahweh, and each Israelite, entering the holy Temple through the "gate of righteousness," was to give his adherence to the *"law of entry"*: "Who shall ascend the hill of the Lord? And who shall stand in the holy place? He who has clean hands and a pure heart, who does not lift his soul to what is false" (Ps. 24, 3-4; cf. 15; Is. 33, 14-16).

Wisdom does not deal with morality. Her work is not so much with the duties of the Covenent as with a preparation of hearts willing to conform to it; it consists less in setting before men ethical and ritualistic demands, and more in developing in them dispositions favorable for dialoging with God. In short, Wisdom was interested in tracing out the portrait or character of the type of man whom personal asceticism and the experience of the sage would bring to maturity.

In this portrait there is nothing static. We know that since its departure from Egypt, the people of Moses always advanced towards the mysterious goal set up by Yahweh. It was the same for the individuals making up the whole people: pilgrims of God, they traveled towards their destiny. And it was exactly this that Wisdom wanted to teach them, viz., to walk with confidence on the "road to God." In order to give them strength on the way, she teaches them the virtues most needed to surmount the difficulties and hardship of the journey.

The sage will first arm himself with *fortitude* and *courage*. And is it not to the *"violent"* that the Gospel will promise the conquest of the Kingdom, i.e., to those with resolute courage? When it paints a picture of the cowardly man, the one always ready to make excuses for stealing away from the task at hand, it is the strong man that Proverbs is indirectly describing: "The sluggard says, 'There is a lion outside! I shall be slain in the streets!'" (22, 13; cf. 26, 13). "The way of the sluggard is overgrown with thorns" (15, 19).

Vainly does he divert his thoughts with empty dreams and

foolish talk (14, 23; 28, 19), his desertion condemns him to misery and death: "The sluggard does not plow in the autumn; he will seek at harvest and have nothing" (20, 4; cf. 13, 4).

He is like the hunter unable to benefit by his catch (12, 27) and the guest who does not have the strength to eat what is put before him (19, 24; cf. 26, 15); both will die of hunger (cf. 20, 13; 19, 15; 11, 16). Spiritual carelessness is comparable to a cowardly spirit at grips with the common problems of every day: "A little sleep, a little slumber, a little folding of the hands to rest, and poverty will come upon you like the robber, and want like the armed man" (24, 33-34).

The sluggard will not enjoy the good things promised by Yahweh. It is even a waste of time to invite such a one to Wisdom's banquet.

Courage alone gains entrance into the kingdom. But what must be said of the lively spirit given over to unruly ambitions? Self-control and temperance must give such a man proper orientation, for the wise man is *master of his own heart*: "A man without self-control is like a city broken into and left without walls" (25, 28). "... every fool will be quarreling" (20, 3).

This is true of envy: "A tranquil mind gives life to the flesh, but passion makes the bones rot" (14, 30). And it is also true of anger: "He who is slow to anger is better than the mighty, and he who rules his spirit than he who takes a city" (16, 32). "The vexation of a fool is known at once, but the prudent man ignores an insult" (12, 16). "Good sense makes a man slow to anger, and it is his glory to overlook an offense" (19, 11).

The wise man preserves peace of soul by refusing to meddle in the quarrels of others: "As charcoal to hot embers and wood to fire, so is the quarrelsome man for kindling strife" (26, 21).

His calm is outstanding, and he is ready to cover up the faults of his neighbor by finding words that bring out peace: "Hatred stirs up strife, but love covers all offenses" (10, 12).

"A soft answer turns away wrath, but a harsh word stirs up anger" (15, 1).

One is not master of himself until he learns how to control his tongue: "The babbling of fools brings ruin" (10, 14). "There is one whose rash words are like sword thrusts, but the tongue of the wise brings healing" (12, 18).

We have only to recall the harm done by the informer: "For lack of wood the fire goes out; and where there is no whisperer, quarreling ceases" (26, 20; cf. 22).

Let us recall the harm done by one who violates a secret: "Argue your case with your neighbor himself, and do not disclose another's secret" (25, 9; cf. 20, 19). "He who forgives an offense seeks love, but he who repeats a matter alienates a friend" (17,9).

Silence is always the best policy: "He who retains his words has knowledge, and he who has a cool spirit is a man of understanding" (17, 27). "Even a fool who keeps silent is considered wise; when he closes his lips, he is deemed intelligent" (17, 28). "He who guards his mouth preserves his life; he who opens wide his lips comes to ruin" (13, 3).

The wise man guards himself against what can make him lose control: gluttony and drunkenness: "Wine is a mocker, strong drink a brawler; and whoever is led astray by it is not wise" (20, 1). "Who has woe? Who has sorrow? Those who tarry long over wine" (23, 29-30). "Do not look at when it is red, and when it sparkles in the cup and goes down smoothly. At the last it bites like a serpent, and stings like an adder" (23, 31-32). "When you sit down to eat with a ruler, observe carefully what is before you; and put a knife to your throat if you are a man given to appetite. Do not desire his delicacies, for they are deceptive food" (23, 1-3).

We see in these the Bible, far from being indulgent towards the powerful, demands of the wise man that solid combination of strength and temperance, for without them man never attains perfection. On the other hand, too many historians easily forget the excesses of the powerful and recount only their bold deeds.

The wise man is to be *faithful* in love just as God is. God's path is straight, and man must walk along it with rectitude. How can the constancy of the divine vocation accommodate itself to hesitancy and deviation? "He who walks in integrity will be delivered, but he who is perverse in his ways will fall into a pit" (28, 18).

One should express himself frankly: "He who winks the eye causes trouble, but he who boldly reproves makes peace" (10, 10). "He who hates, dissembles with his lips and harbors deceit in his heart" (26, 24).

One should keep his promises: "Like clouds and wind without rain is a man who boasts of a gift he does not give" (25, 14).

Falsehood and cheating are to be detested: "The thoughts of the righteous are just; the counsels of the wicked are treacherous" (12, 5). "The way of the guilty is crooked, but the conduct of the pure is right" (21, 8). The *yes* of the wise man is *yes*, his *no* is *no*; he is "just."

As temperance disciplines strength, so *prudence* moderates justice; righteousness is not synoymous with stubbornness. Jesus recommends that the prudence of the serpent be joined to the simplicity of the dove. The wise man always proceeds with prudence: "Blessed is the man who fears the Lord; but he who hardens his heart will fall into calamity" (28, 14). He does not expose himself thoughtlessly to danger; he does not take unnecessary risks: "A prudent man sees danger and hides himself; but the simple go on, and suffer for it" (22, 3; cf. 27, 12). "It is a snare for a man to say rashly, 'It is holy,' and to reflect only after making his vows" (20, 25). "He who gives surety for a stranger will smart for it" (11, 15; cf. 6, 1-5; 27, 13; 20, 16; 22, 26-27; etc.).

It is prudence not to importune friends; it is better for others to seek you out: "Let your foot be seldom in your neighbor's house, lest he become weary of you and hate you" (25, 17).

Fortitude, temperance, prudence, and justice are the four cardinal virtues which insure perfect balance in man, placing him in God's hands and surrendering him to God's transcendent action. The Israelite, thanks to these virtues, prepares the Christian of tomorrow. He will live in this world without being of it. Fully conscious of his responsibility to society, he is sufficiently detached from it to be able to hear and answer the divine call. Though he is above his earthly condition, he does not avoid his duties, but remains always available for the sacrifice to which God invites him. This may develop into the total gift of self, the heroic abnegation of love. Though not yet this perfect, the disciple of Wisdom will at least be *malleable to the work of the divine hands.* He will present himself to society as an *amiable* and *generous* man, spreading peace, joy, and health.

This wise man does not have the odious qualities of the misanthrope. True, he does not hesitate to correct his brother, never stooping to flattery; yet he is loved: "He who rebukes a man will afterward find more favor than he who flatters with his tongue" (28, 23).

He realizes that obsequiousness rings a false note: "He who blesses his neighbor with a loud voice, rising early in the morning, will be counted as cursing" (27, 14).

He knows that empty praise fills one with disgust: "It is not good to eat much honey, so be sparing of complimentary words" (25, 27).

The wise man tempers his candor with sweetness; the amount of honey given out is just right: "Pleasant words are like a honeycomb, sweetness to the soul and health to the body" (16, 24).

This sweetness comes not from an exaggerated or false kindness but from a benevolence of the best alloy: "The mind of the wise man makes his speech judicious, and adds persuasiveness to his lips" (16, 23).

What is there which goodness cannot accomplish, whether it expresses itself through word or look! "The light of the eyes rejoices the heart" (15, 30). "A soft answer turns away wrath" (15, 1). "A soft tongue will break a bone" (25, 15).

The charm of the wise man flows mostly from his kindness, and when it is accompanied with liberality it brings many friends, especially sychophants: "Many seek the favor of a generous man, and everyone is a friend to a man who gives gifts" (19, 6).

Jesus will say, "*Make friends for yourselves with the mammon of iniquity.*" Proverbs advises against stinginess in giving if one is desirous of gaining a favor or disarming the powerful: "A man's gift makes room for him and brings him before great men" (18, 16). "A gift in secret averts anger; and a bribe in the bosom, strong wrath" (21, 14); but better still when there is question of alleviating misery: "Happy is he who is kind to the poor" (14, 21). These poor, who find no friends (19, 4 & 7) and whose lot one is never sure of not sharing some day (21, 13), have a right to compassion. Are they not brothers of the wise man, children of the same Father? "He who mocks the poor insults his Maker; he who is glad at calamity will not go unpunished" (17, 5). "He who oppresses a poor man insults his Maker, but he who is kind to the needy honors him" (14, 31).

Remembering that "he who hates unjust gain will prolong his days" (28, 16), far from hoarding like a miser "the righteous gives and does not hold back" (21, 26). He knows that "though one man gives freely, yet grows all the richer; another withholds what he should give, and suffers want" (11, 24).

The Gospel will add other teachings on justice and fraternal love; these will be extensions of the old wisdom of Israel. On this point there is just as much continuity as there is a break between the two Testaments. In the Old Testament the just man had learned not to rejoice over the enemy's fall (24, 17), for vengeance was the Lord's: "Does not he who weighs the heart perceive it? Does not he who keeps watch over your soul know it, and will he not requite man according to his works?" (24, 12).

He had learned to exercise mercy towards the enemy: "If

your enemy is hungry, give him bread to eat; and if he is thirsty, give him water to drink" (25, 21).

*   *   *

The more we consider this wise man, the more attractive he becomes. Comparing him to his Egyptian model we find him more serious, his language less flowery, and song rises less spontaneously to his lips. However, for one who does not exteriorize himself in the affected ways of the courtier, his joy is much deeper. All through Israel's long and painful history, joy abounds in its soul: "A cheerful heart is a good medicine, but a downcast spirit dries up the bones" (17, 22).

One could not advance without the virtues extolled by Wisdom; he would even come to a standstill in their absence, for one must be sustained by strong joy which aids him in overcoming fatigue and discouragement: "A man's spirit will endure sickness, but a broken spirit who can bear? (18, 14). "He who sings songs to a heavy heart is like one who takes off a garment on a cold day, and like vinegar on a wound" (25, 20).

The just man draws joy from Wisdom who never fails him. How can he cease drinking from her? "All the days of the afflicted are evil, but the cheerful heart has a continual feast" (15, 15).

The Wisdom of Proverbs is full of harmony: plunging her roots into the most ancient civilizations, she has grown bathed in an eternal light. She will soon be excelled, but she is nonetheless the living and generous tree that will be grafted and will bear much fruit some day. Thus she merits more from us than our respectful esteem. Her doctrine can still be the inspiration of useful examinations of conscience. Anyone desirous of setting foot on the royal road of the Lord can take her as guide in order to acquire that moral balance such a commitment demands.

After all, is she not the one who prepared the spontaneous and victorious consent of the Annunciation, the model of our own most humble and fruitful assents to God's will? And is it not her serene joy that will develop into that radiant smile of the *Magnificat?*

## C.- THE FRUITS OF WISDOM

If the practice of the moral Law is sanctioned by the intervention of the supreme Legislator, retribution is applied to definite acts which are situated in time. But Wisdom, we repeat again, is not morality: her fruits ripen slowly, nourished by the continuous conduct of a whole life-time. Morality sets up a catalogue of rewards and punishments; Wisdom enumerates the benefits of dealing with her. Thus it is wrong for anyone to have sought, in the question of retribution, the key-problem of the Wisdom Books of Israel.

One should seek the *company of Wisdom* for herself alone. We cannot buy her because she is above all earthly goods, whether it be a question of power or riches: "A wise man is mightier than a strong man" (24, 5). "Take my instruction instead of silver, and knowledge rather than choice gold; for Wisdom is better than jewels, and all that you may desire cannot compare with her" (8, 10-11; cf. 16, 16).

What she procures for her followers is knowledge of God: "If you seek understanding like silver and search for it as for a hidden treasure, then you will understand the fear of the Lord and find knowledge of God" (2, 4-5).

Since this is so, why is it that we do not attach ourselves to Wisdom as we would to a spouse? "Say to Wisdom, 'You are my sister,' and call insight your intimate friend" (7, 4).

When we surrender ourself to Wisdom and her guidance, we find a delightful and sure companion. She will guide us to the end of our journey: "Her ways are the ways of pleasantness, and all her paths are peace" (3, 17; cf. 2, 10).

The reason for this is that while we are always travelers on the march we attain the object of our pursuit. Our traveling is not an aimless wandering. Does not Yahweh promise Israel that it will "enter into his repose," provided it is faithful? (cf. Ps. 95, 11). Was not the land flowing with milk and honey the termination of the journey for the Hebrews of Moses' time? Centuries later that great unknown prophet whose message was incorporated in the Book of Isaiah will invite his companions in exile to the land of their fathers where they will find wheat, wine, and milk in abundance (Is. 55, 1).

Is this an echo to that last invitation which, in the introduction to the Book of Proverbs, the Lady who incarnates Wisdom invites her followers into her house where her table is prepared? "She has slaughtered her beasts, she has mixed her wine, and she has set her table" (9, 2).

Perhaps she still dreams of bringing them back to that lost paradise where living waters flow, the sources of life, viz., understanding and the fear of Yahweh (14, 27; cf. 16, 22). Having quenched his thirst there, the disciple becomes the fountain for the passer-by: "The teaching of the wise is a fountain of life, that one may avoid the snares of death" (13, 14; cf. 10, 11). "The words of a man's mouth are deep waters; the fountain of wisdom is a gushing stream" (18, 4).

Or perhaps Wisdom has in mind to have them find once more that Eden where the tree of life set up its eternal branches: "She is a tree of life to those who lay hold of her" (3, 18). Nourished with its fruits, justice and mercy, the wise man spreads abroad the essence of this marvelous tree: "The fruit of the righteous is a tree of life" (11, 30). "A gentle tongue is a tree of life" (15, 4).

Whatever her design, this august Lady does not simply promise the reward of good works. The image of the meal is indicative enough of the natural consequence of either acceptance or refusal on the part of the passer-by. Thus, the impious, instead of Wisdom's bread, prefer that of their errors: ". . . therefore they shall eat the fruit of their way" (1, 31); they condemn themselves to eating "the bread of wickedness" and drinking the "wine of violence" (4, 17). They go to the feast of Folly not realizing she will serve them deadly illusions: "[he does not know] that her guests are the depths of Sheol" (9, 18). Again, "The simple are killed by their turning away, and the complacence of fools destroys them" (1, 32).

Man chooses life or death, depending on whether he seats himself at the table of Wisdom or Folly.

✿ ✿ ✿

It is fitting, however, we specify here what the Bible means by *life* and *death*. If only we could define the meaning of these two essential words! When Wisdom promises life to her disciples, she fills their heart with a hope the riches of which defies exact description. What one can say of it, at least, is that this life permits man to utilize to the full his "potential" and in this way to accomplish *fully* his destiny without the possibility of death's coming to break prematurely the course of that life. He will have truly lived who, attaining the ideal number of his years, will be extinguished like a dried-out wick, which will never be able to be brought to life again by any external breath. Just as the wheat is not harvested until it is ripe, so he will not descend into Sheol until he has *"fulfilled his days."*

Now, if the "beauty of old men is their grey hairs" (20, 29), it is to the wise man that "length of days" is promised since "a hoary head is a crown of glory, it is gained in a righteous life" (16, 31; cf. 3, 16). Old age is not given to the wicked: ". . . lawlessness takes away lives" (11, 30; cf. 10, 27). "The mouth of the wicked counsels violence" (10, 6).

This plenitude of life is not measured simply by years; it supposes a *stability* and a *security*, without which it would not be realized. Did not Yahweh make the solid mass rise from the chaotic Abyss? He built it up like an unshakable fortress in the face of the fury of the sea monsters. Such too is the house built by Wisdom (14, 1): it rests upon a solid foundation (24, 3), while that of the wicked will be destroyed (14, 1), either through foolishness (14, 1) or through Yahweh's anger (15, 25). The house of the just lasts (12, 7), as the vine planted by Yahweh in Canaan: "The root of the righteous will never be moved" (12, 3; cf. 12, 12).

This stability was assured in the primitive desert community only through *sharing in tribal life;* anyone who was cut off from it was condemned to death: deprived of support, he no longer had anyone to defend or avenge him. Later this belonging to a group is concretized by the granting of a part of the heritage in the land of Canaan: to live is no longer to dwell in a community but to live in the same land. It is thus understood by Wisdom: "For the upright will inhabit the land, and men of security will remain in it; but the wicked will be cut off from the land" (2, 21-22).

Existence in either case is no longer conceived apart from belonging to a definite "milieu"; the desperate flight of Cain on an earth that refuses to hold him is perhaps nothing but the worst aspect of death. Proverbs points out the tragic character of this "excommunication." "If a man is burdened with the blood of another, let him be a fugitive until death; let no one help him" (28, 17). He roams the earth like a hunted beast, always on the watch: "The wicked flee when no one pursues" (28, 1). It is a miserable existence. As the plant clings to the rock seeking protection against the storm, so man takes refuge within a community established upon a definite soil (27, 8). Anxieties and insecurity eat into the heart and deprive its existence of any meaning. Job was well aware of this bitter existence when he stated: "My days are swifter than a weaver's shuttle, and come to their end without hope" (Job 7, 6).

Hebrew expresses by the same word the ideas of "fast" and "light": the days of Job have the lightness of the empty ear of corn. How can one live in the midst of anxiety? Work and rest which give meaning to life are impossible for one who does not have a feeling of security (cf. 19, 23).

Now the fool does not remain deaf in vain to Wisdom's teaching; he will gain experience from it: ". . . when panic strikes you like a storm, and your calamity comes like a whirlwind" (1, 27). It will then be night for him when "his lamp will be put out in utter darkness" (20, 20; cf. 24, 20). "The way of the wicked is like a deep darkness; they do not know over what they stumble" (4, 19).

On the other hand, what fullness of life is promised to the wise man! "Then you will walk on your way securely and your foot will not stumble. If you sit down you will not be afraid; when you lie down your sleep will be sweet. Do not be afraid of sudden panic, or of the ruin of the wicked when it comes" (3, 23-25).

Under Wisdom's guidance: ". . . a righteous man sings and rejoices" (29, 6), for his route is free, bathed in the marvelous light that Yahweh made shine at the first instant of creation, forcing darkness back and casting out dangers: "But the path of the righteous is like the light of dawn, which shines brighter and brighter until the full day" (4, 18).

Without stability and security, human life, then, is without consistency. It is necessary, if life is to take on its full worth, that the *profound aspirations of the heart be realized*: "Hope deferred makes the heart sick, but a desire fulfilled is a tree of life" (13, 12).

The disciple of Wisdom will see them satisfied: "The hope of the righteous man is gladness" (10, 28). "The desire of the righteous will be granted" (10, 24). "No ill befalls the righteous" (12, 21). "The righteous has enough to satisfy his appetite (13, 25).

If the dreams of the fool are sources of deception, and if

"the expectation of the wicked comes to naught" (10, 28; cf. 10, 24; 11, 7, 23), the future of the wise man is filled with promise: "If you find wisdom, there will be a future, and your hope will not be cut off" (24, 14; cf. 23, 18).

One would expect from Israel's Wisdom an explanation of the nature of happiness in which the just man's life is to develop and his hopes to be realized. But she gives this problem no consideration. She will leave its development to the best minds of Greece; and it is only later on that she will draw from their meditations. For the moment she does not withdraw from the customary perspectives that limit her horizon to what man can desire on earth, viz., health, fortune, honor, friendship.

We must, nevertheless, observe that, as limited as is this horizion, it is not closed: just as the traveler sees, in proportion as he walks, the end of his road receding, it is the same with Wisdom. If, for example, Wisdom lets it be understood that the goods of fortune assure independence, security, and consideration (10, 15; 18, 11; 19, 4; 22, 7), she observes, on the contrary, how relative their value is: "Better is a little with the fear of the Lord than great treasure and trouble with it. Better is a dinner with herbs where love is than a fatted ox and hatred with it" (15, 16-17). "Better is a little with righteousness than great revenue with injustice" (16, 8; cf. 28, 6).

Although Wisdom does not give them a glimpse of a new heaven and a new earth, she already opens the hearts of her disciples to a hope which as yet their understanding is unable to conceive. Perhaps this is why she does not define the nature of happiness which she is constantly promising. She holds out to her listener the hope of infinity which even death's prospect cannot dampen and which she softens by the thought that the just man will live on his reputation and his posterity: "The memory of the righteous is a blessing" (10, 7). "A righteous man walks in his integrity, blessed are his sons afer him" (20, 7).

Many centuries are to pass before the God of Abraham, Isaac, and Jacob will appear no longer as the God of the dead but of the living, raising his children to make them live on with him eternally. When giving the wise man the promise of life, the realization of his aspirations, and the perfect fulfillment of his destiny, Wisdom is simply transposing to the level of the individual Yahweh's oath to the people: Israel will find life only under the guiding hand of God; withdrawal from his hand spells death. The sage, like Israel, could not understand the infinite meaning of this promise of life and death. What each understood very clearly was the necessity of total surrender to the hand of God who sees everything: "Sheol and Abaddon lie open before the Lord, how much more the hearts of men!" (15, 11). As Master of the destiny of both individuals and peoples, he guides them with his infallible Wisdom: "Many are the plans of the mind of a man, but it is the purpose of the Lord that will be established" (19, 21). In his omnipotence he is the surest of ramparts: "The name of the Lord is a strong tower; the righteous man runs into it and is safe" (18, 10). "He who trusts in the Lord is safe" (29, 25). He deigns to hear and answer the prayers of the just: "The Lord is far from the wicked, but he hears the prayers of the righteous" (15, 29). He grants him both favor and friendship: "A good man obtains favor from the Lord" (12, 2). "Men of blameless ways are his delight" (11, 20; cf. 15, 8, 9; 16, 7; 22, 11).

*　*　*

Must we, like others, condemn the Old Testament as being materialistic in its views? Atfer all, its perspectives in the Wisdom Books lie on this side, on an earthly destiny. Is it to be blamed if its myopia does not allow it to distinguish man's last ends? Is the grandeur of its message lessened? What it never ceases to affirm is the solicitude of a God who remains undoubtedly deaf to the desires of his people but conducts them with certainty towards a goal the secret of which he alone knows; who, if he finds this people docile, will give to its being the greatest development.

Through this conviction a thousand times repeated, Israel's Wisdom held herself at an equal distance from two opposed pitfalls into which human thought has too often fallen. In advance she rejected, under all its forms, the ancient Promethean dream of man who, through his resources alone, would give to the world its completion. On the other hand, Wisdom refused to cause a miscarriage in a humanity in labor over its imaginary grandeur which would be based on too premature a hope of life beyond the grave. As far removed from a God without man of Islam as of man without God of Marxism, Israel's Wisdom proclaims the necessity of the assumption of man by his God who will one day find his completion in the indissoluble union with God.

### D.- WISDOM, DOOR OF THE COVENANT

No one enters the New Covenant introduced by Jeremiah without first having made a personal choice. To incline hearts to make this choice, it is the Wisdom of Solomon's court that offers her help to those who are seeking life. Her help is not only useful, but indispensable; a man would not succeed in committing himself without her aid.

In truth, neither the people as a whole nor the individual chooses God. Each makes the response to the divine invitation. Invited to enjoy the experience of Yahweh's hand, the people and the individual have only to prove themselves responsive. The prophets patiently recalled this truth to Israel; Wisdom, in her turn, presents herself to her eventual disciples as the Lady who invites them to sit at her table. Far different from the schools of philosophy that offer themselves for the free choice of individuals, it is Wisdom who calls: "She has sent out her maids to call from the highest places in the town, 'Whoever is simple, let him turn in here! To him who is without sense she says, 'Come, eat of my bread and drink of the wine I have mixed'" (9, 3-5).

It would seem we have nothing here differentiating the Wisdom of Israel from that of the ancient civilizations. In Egypt, for example, or in Babylon, wisdom was essentially traditional: the old transmitted the experience they acquired throughout their lives. Collections of maxims frequently had as authors fathers who were anxious to have their sons follow in the steps that led them to success.

Let us see, however, where exactly the originality of Israel's Wisdom resides. In Egypt the children were expected to lay claim to inheriting paternal knowledge as a thing most precious in their patrimony. In Israel Wisdom is presented always as a free gift, as the individual makes the same response to her as did the people as a whole to the divine Covenant at Sinai. It is not the possession of the chosen few, neither can one claim it as his own. Wisdom offers her riches to all freely; her audience is as limitless as that of Yahweh himself. And her appeal, like that of the prophets, makes itself heard wherever the crowds gather together: "Wisdom cries aloud in the streets; in the markets she raises her voice; on the top of the walls she cries out; at the entrance to the city gates she speaks" (1, 20-21). "On the heights beside the way, in the paths she takes her stand; beside the gates in front of the town, at the entrance of the portals she cries aloud: 'To you, O men, I call, and my cry is to the sons of men'" (8, 2-4).

Not only does this universal call not correspond to any legitimate demand of man, but not one here below merits the attention which Wisdom wishes to give him. Just as formerly Yahweh picked up the daughter of Israel bathed in her own blood (Ez. 16, 6) and did this out of pure goodness, so also Wisdom bends down to the foolish ones who are already on the path of perdition: "O simple ones, will you love being simple? How long will scoffers delight in their scoffing?" (1, 22).

*   *   *

Standing at the crossroads to turn men from error and crime, Wisdom takes up the themes of the prophets, especially the kernel of Jeremiah's message: "Be converted!" If Yahweh former-ly took in hand a rebellious people, Wisdom now tries to draw away a perverted humanity from sin: "For Wisdom will come into your heart, and knowledge will be pleasant to your soul; discretion will watch over you; understanding will guard you; delivering you from the way of evil, from men of perverted speech, who forsake the paths of uprightness to walk in the way of darkness" (2, 10-13).

This strong language is not the language of human prudence. We cannot confuse it with the language of philosophers, no matter how great their aims may be. This language is used be-cause Wisdom is not limited to spreading an earthly science; in her teaching it is the very voice of God that is heard: "For the Lord gives Wisdom; from his mouth come knowledge and understanding" (2, 6).

Wisdom's appeal comes directly from Yahweh's merciful love and it is this which makes it gratuitous Wisdom.

As God's mouth-piece on a level with prophecy, Wisdom is created to express all the divine demands and to expect an obedience to them which is neither weak nor faltering. One who has chosen in favor of her is not to go back on his word. Like the God of the Covenant, Wisdom does not allow one to take sides, "to go limping with two different opinions," as Elijah expressed it (1 Kgs. 18, 21). "Keep hold of instruction, do not let her go; guard her for she is your life. Do not enter the path of the wicked, and do not walk in the way of evil men. Avoid it; do not go on it; turn away from it and pass on" (4, 13-15).

"Let your eyes look directly forward, and your gates be straight before you. Take heed to the path of your feet, then all your ways will be sure. Do not swerve to the right or to the left; turn your foot away from evil" (4, 25-27).

With Deuteronomy Wisdom will repeat: "Do not forget, and do not turn away from the words of my mouth" (4, 5).

And, certainly, there is no question here of an obedience that is more or less passive or even constrained like that of a schoolboy's submission. The disciple will not assimilate Wisdom's teachings in spite of himself: "If you seek it like silver and search for it as for hidden treasures; then you will understand the fear of the Lord" (2, 4-5).

His ears and his heart will receive it hungrily: "My son, be attentive to my words; incline your ear to my sayings. Let them not escape from your sight; keep them within your heart" (4, 20-21).

The disciple of Wisdom will fear nothing more than losing a treasure so dearly purchased: does not Wisdom, as Jesus will do later on, command him to guard it with great vigilance? "Happy the man who listens to me, who day after day watches at my gates to guard the portals" (8, 34).

The counsels of Wisdom, like Yahweh's words, are gathered with love in the depths of one's heart: "Bind them upon your heart always; tie them about your neck" (6, 21). "Keep my commandments and live, keep my teachings as the apple of your eye; bind them on your fingers, write them on the tablet of your heart" (7, 2-3).

It is not enough to open one's understanding to them: Wisdom is not less demanding than Yahweh whose hand wishes to embrace man totally. It is to *keeping guard over his heart* that the disciple is invited above all else: "Keep your heart with all vigilance; for from it flow the springs of life" (4, 23). "Blessed are the pure of heart," the Gospel says.

Man must respond to Wisdom's gratuitous invitation with the total gift of himself. The reason for this is that his dealing with her is placed under the sign of *love*: "I love those who love me, and those who seek me diligently find me" (8, 17).

Yahweh covers his elect with his wings: "He stores up sound wisdom for the upright; he is a shield to those who walk in integrity, guarding the paths of justice and preserving the way of the saints" (2, 7-8).

Wisdom acts likewise: "For Wisdom will come into your heart and knowledge will be pleasant to your soul; discretion will watch over you; understanding will guard you; delivering you from the way of evil, from men of perverted speech" (2, 10-12).

The just man, whose sleep Wisdom watches over, will find her ready to carry on the interrupted dialogue upon his rising, and to teach him her doctrine which even a whole life-time cannot exhaust: "When you walk they will lead you, and when you lie down, they will watch over you; and when you awake, they will talk with you" (6, 22).

Does not this mutual love remind us of the story of Yahweh and Israel so frequently brought out by the prophets? of that quasi-carnal union, the image of which will be used by our mystics? They will be accused of hysteria. However, this image which has contributed so much to bringing out the sanctity of marriage is the best one can find to express the intimacy of the soul with God: "Say to Wisdom, 'You are my sister'" (7, 4).

This wonderful idyll is acquainted with storms. The one between Yahweh and his people had been troubled by many dramatic episodes, in which the spouse's infidelity merited many severe lessons for her. Yahweh, in spite of his love for Israel, never allowed himself to become a slave to its caprices: whenever the chosen people withdrew from the divine embrace, it condemned itself to wandering in darkness and stretching forth its arms to the Bridegroom who is both unseen and silent. A similar disgrace is reserved for those who betray Wisdom: "Because I called you and you refused to listen, have stretched out my hand and no one heeded, and you have ignored all my counsel and would have none of my reproof, I also will laugh at your calamity; I will mock when panic strikes you, when panic strikes you like a storm, and your calamity comes like a whirlwind, when distress and anguish come upon you. Then they will call upon me, but I will not answer; and they will seek me diligently but will not find me" ( 1, 24-28 ).

\* \* \*

In short, Yahweh's conduct towards the individual is comparable to that towards the people chosen in the desert. Whether it be collective or individual, the commitment required by the divine call always demands an *intermediary*. No one can stand before God alone. Moses did not climb Mount Sinai as an individual but as leader of the people; herein lies the difference between personages presented by the Bible and the Koran. Israel, later on, will need the strong rod of the prophets to gather together her scattered sheep. And Wisdom will be for the individual the indispensable mediatrix who, after having made him well aware of his vocation, will sustain him in it. She will introduce him into divine intimacy. She will, in a word, be the door to the New Covenant.

We are tempted to say here what the Fathers will one day say of the Church; "No one can have God for Father who does not have Wisdom for mother."

### E.- EVE AND MARY

"Whoever is simple let him turn in here" (9, 4) is the cry of both Wisdom and Folly to the passer-by. But the former speak strongly to the foolish: "Come, eat of my bread and drink of the wine that I have mixed. Leave simpleness, and live, and walk in the way of insight" (9, 5-6). Folly, on the other hand, whispers her deceitful promises: "Stolen water is sweet, and bread eaten in secret is pleasant" (9, 17). She does not speak of life, and this with good reason: "Man does not know that the dead are there, that her guests are in the depths of Sheol" (9, 18).

The "stolen" waters that do not satisfy are opposed to the healthful waters which one draws from his own well: "Let your fountains be blessed" (5, 8); to the dismal feast of the evil hostess (could one expect anything better from her, for "a foolish woman is noisy; she is wanton and knows no shame" 9, 13) is opposed the substantial meal which the noble mistress of the house in her clear-sighted diligence has provided. She has spared nothing in order to treat her guests well in a house where everything breathes order, abundance, and security (9, 1-2).

Security: though: "Wisdom builds her house, folly tears it down with her own hands" (14, 1). Of her own house it is said: "... her house sinks down to death" (2, 18), while on the solid foundation laid by prudence (cf. 24, 3), Wisdom finds that perfect stability which Yahweh assured the world at its creation. Israel has a sure proof of this in the Temple solidly built and set upon the holy mount.

               ✿   ✿   ✿

Here we have two antithetical figures, one is that of the *ideal woman,* the other, the *prostitute.* They offer concurrently *life* and *death*: "Drink water from your own cistern, flowing water from your own well. Should your springs be scattered abroad, streams of water in the streets? Let them be for yourself alone, and not for strangers with you. Let your fountain be blessed, and rejoice in the wife of your youth" (5, 15-18). "Why should you be infatuated, my son, with a loose woman and embrace the bosom of an adventuress?" (5, 20). "For the lips of a loose woman drip honey, and her speech is smoother than oil; but in the end she is bitter as wormwood, sharp as a two-edged sword. Her feet go down to death; her steps follow the path of Sheol" (5, 3-5).

With the prostitute the fruit of one's labor is wasted (5, 10), one's vitality is ruined and honor lost (2, 18); but the faithful wife does "her husband good, and not harm, all the days of her life" (31, 12).

Is there question here of Folly and Wisdom, of the wanton woman and the good wife? It is not without reason that we have set these texts side by side: there is a curious correlation in Scripture between the one and the other: a correlation so close — we shall explain it later — that the one seems to bring up the other.

Fidelity and adultery, Wisdom and Folly, two Women solicit the attention of men. In the second we easily recognize the ancient prostitute, Israel, who formerly ran off wildly in pursuit of "strange" or "unknown" divinities and powers: it was she who caused the Hebrews to lose, along with the heritage of their fathers, the fruit of their own works.

Alongside this pitiful figure that monopolized the scene for so long a time, there is another full of nobility and purity, the virgin Israel, who seeks to gather her children under her wings as does a hen her chicks.

Is there need to underline the novelty? The Bible, until then, was acquainted only with the tormented image of the faithless one depicted by the prophets: it was she whom Yahweh, after having cast her away, willed to gain back again: "And there (in the desert) she shall answer as in the days of her youth, as at the time when she came out of the land of Egypt" (Hos. 2, 15). "For the Lord has called you like a wife forsaken and grieved in spirit, like a wife of youth when she is cast off, says your God" (Is. 54, 6).

Thus, after the Exile, when the New Covenant predicted by Jeremiah is already in its incipient stage, the Jews will have to decide between regression to a past filled with wanderings and sin — Folly — and the coming of a new world, lovingly abandoned to the divine will — Wisdom.

The experience of the Return had shown that, though the

new people was formed in the decisive trial of individual fidelities, the old condemned Israel nonetheless survived in the obstinacy of those who, deaf to the lessons of adversity, persisted in withdrawing themselves from the hand of Yahweh. The struggle is on now between the votaries of a rebellious past and the pious reformers — lawyers and sages, prophets and psalmists. This dualism which we shall come upon in the doctrine of the *"two ways"* professed at Qumran, begins to enter biblical thought; Israel will become progressively conscious of this co-existence of good and evil, as the choice becomes more costly and dramatic.

❊   ❊   ❊

It is not by chance that this opposition between refusal and acceptance is illustrated in our wisdom literature by the contrast between Folly and Wisdom; neither is it by chance that these writings made use of two female figures to incarnate the powers of good and evil, the fortunes of life and the dangers of death. Is it not in Woman that yes and no are best expressed, obedience and revolt, fidelity and betrayal? That is why the problem of Woman is identified, in great measure, with that of Wisdom.

We easily accuse the Old Testament of being anti-woman; and texts are not lacking which seem to prove it. Call to mind the characteristics applied to the shrew — the woman shorn of that delicacy which goes to make up so much of her charm. Although these traits are picturesquely presented in Proverbs, nevertheless the book simply agrees with what has been described in literature: "A wife's quarreling is a continual dripping of rain" (19, 13; cf. 27, 15). "It is better to live in a corner of the housetop than in the house shared with a contentious woman" (21, 9; cf. 21, 19; 25, 24). "Like a gold ring in a swine's snout is a beautiful woman without discretion" (11, 22).

More impressive is the long list of portraits in which the woman of the Bible appears malevolent. After Eve, temptation took on many faces: we have only to think of the wife of Job or

Tobit; in the prosperous days of Egypt, the wife of Putiphar; shortly after the Exodus, the daughters of Moab; under the Judges, Dalilah; at the time of the kings, the wives and concubines of Solomon, or the sinister princesses of Tyre, Jezabel and Athaly. A disturbing lot, and the prostitute of Proverbs is a worthy companion of them all: "With much seductive speech she persuades him; with her smooth talk she compels him. All at once he follows her, as an ox to the slaughter, or a stag is caught fast till an arrow pierces its entrails; as a bird rushes into a snare; he does not know that it will cost him his life" (7, 21-23).

But we meet the opposite type of woman in the Bible. Some noble characters are left in the haziness of the background too often to suit us; but this is explained by saying that it is not women who weave history but men. As for those who emerge from the shadows, their traits, we aver, never appear to us as absolutely pure, whether there be question of the beautiful wives of the patriarchs, or even such heroines as Judith.

All this is true; but there is the description of the delicate and fine visage of the prudent wife about whom the sage speaks — the one who is found always at home: "A good wife is the crown of her husband" (12, 4). "Her husband is known in the gates" (31, 23; cf. 11, 16). "Charm is deceitful and beauty is vain, but the woman who fears the Lord is to be praised" (31, 30). "Strength and dignity are her clothing, and she laughs at the days to come" (31, 25). "Her children rise up and call her blessed; her husband also, and he praises her" (31, 28).

Though woman can be the cause of death, she is also the source of happiness, security, and honor, on condition that she seek perfection in Wisdom: "She opens her mouth with wisdom, and the teaching of kindness is on her tongue" (31, 26).

Like Wisdom, she too is a rare pearl. Without being as undeceived as Qoheleth who will cry out bitterly: "One man among a thousand I found, but a woman among all these I have not found" (Eccles. 7, 28), the wise man of Proverbs says simply: "A good wife who can find?" (31, 10).

We must be on our guard, however: it is not from contempt of woman that this severity proceeds, but from the very high ideal that the Bible has made of woman.

If, in fact, like Wisdom, the perfect Wife is rare, she is priceless. Her traits, like those of Wisdom, are of such perfection that only the hand of God can mold them; which comes to the same as saying that the one and the other are a gift from God; that neither the one nor the other are explained without the mystery of grace: "For the Lord gives wisdom" (2, 6), and "A prudent wife is from the Lord" (19, 14).

How can we fail to be struck by this parallelism so insistently repeated and which will stand out more strongly as time goes on? How can we fail to be struck by the connection between the real in which man seeks himself, and the ideal after which he aspires? Is there no connection between Wisdom from whom God borrows a voice and woman through whom humanity responds? Perhaps it is because ideal humanity is incarnated in the ideal Woman. The best of men dream of her because God has planted in their heart a longing for her.

In proportion as Wisdom's visage becomes more delineated, that of woman becomes more refined. This twofold progress will be more closely linked to a progress in a religious teaching which will deepen the nature and quality of Israel's relationship with its God.

For example, the idea of conjugal fidelity so highly prized by the wise man of Proverbs owes much more to the invectives of the prophets against the religious prostitution of Israel than it does to the detailed precepts of a legislation which was powerless to condemn polygamy. Ezekiel concludes his indictment against Samaria and Judah, the two sisters whom Jahweh had espoused, with the following merciless warning to Israel's women: "Thus will I put an end to lewdness in the land, that all women may take warning and not commit lewdness as you have done" (Ezek. 23, 48).

Inversely, Proverbs presents the wife who betrays her husband as being unfaithful even to God: "She forsakes the companion of her youth and forgets the covenant of her God" (2, 17).

The attitude of each of Palestine's daughters is a reflection of Israel's fidelity. This explains why the teaching in Proverbs passes so frequently from the theme of wisdom to that of fidelity in marriage: "My son, be attentive to my wisdom, incline your ear to understanding; that you may keep discretion and your lips may guard knowledge" (5, 1-2). "Call insight your intimate friend; to preserve you from the loose woman, from the adventuress with her smooth words" (7, 4-5).

This is so becuse in the Bible the relationship between the sign and the thing signified is not an artificial construction of the mind: the two realities set in parallel interpenetrate and "promote" each other. We have a good example of this here: the fidelity of the wife, the fruit of Wisdom, and Wisdom which instructs humanity in fidelity to God.

Every human soul is invited to realize the *vocation of woman*. What is asked of the soul is not initiative and strength, for these are man's endowments, but rather the *yes* and the *no* which contain woman's destiny. Woman's whole dignity is not to be found in great achievements, nor in passive resignation as Islam would have it, but in the *total gift of self* constantly repeated. This gift of self involves a total commitment through the mind, will, heart, and all the living powers of one's being. When a religious system exalts its heroines, it does so in vain; it has not understood woman's real grandeur. No matter how elevated its teaching may be, it falls short of the divine dialogue, remaining either too human or too inhuman.

This is why the wise man, awaiting the New Israel's advent, ardently invokes the coming of Woman-Wisdom in his prayers. She will transform the world through her uncompromising righteousness and unspotted purity. The soul of Israel's daughters is formed already in the light of this ideal image. The time approaches when this soul will find in the Virgin of Nazareth the perfection of beauty. Then the Woman will rise up in her brilliance and serve henceforth as a model for all her sisters: "And a great sign appeared in the heavens, a woman clothed with the sun . . ." (Rev. 12, 1).

*  *  *

In short, the idyll of Yahweh and Israel will continue to haunt Jewish thought. Far from being a simple metaphor, it clothes two living and complementary realities with its eloquent analogy. The comparison prepares hearts to accept the ideal of Christian marriage which is the foundation of the new society. "As the Church is subject to Christ, so let wives be subject to their husbands in all things" (Eph. 5, 24). "Husbands, love your wives as Christ loved the Church" (5, 25). Responsive to God's call, man sits at the table of either Wisdom or Folly, thus becoming a son of the one or the other. Two women bargain for him: the famous prostitute, herself mother of "harlots and of the earth's abominations" (Rev. 17, 5), the other the new Eve: ". . . she is clothed with the sun, with the moon at her feet, and on her head a crown of twelve stars" (Rev. 17, 1).

Wisdom is the "new Jerusalem, coming down out of the heavens from God, prepared as a bride adorned for her husband" (Rev. 21, 2).

Man must make a choice between these two, just as formerly Abraham had to choose between the opulent and vain security he will leave at Ur and the unknown paths which will lead him to the Canaan of Promise. To enter a new world, each is called upon by God to tear himself away from the past. Obeying Yahweh, Abraham consented to walk alone towards unknown lands while his distant descendant will not cease to advance towards death if he be attracted to Folly, or towards life if he attaches himself to Wisdom. He will be formed in the womb of either Eve or Mary!

F.- WISDOM AND THE CREATED UNIVERSE

This Wisdom is not like other wisdoms of the past. She prepares men's hearts and introduces the people of the Old Covenant into that of the New. She is identified with the faithful virgin, the New Israel. She is not, however, like other wisdoms, but she is a gift which proceeds from Yahweh's liberality and love.

She does not appear on the earth as an accidental good. Although she is superior to the world, she is no stranger to it; for nothing in existence escapes her observation. She exercises her sovereign empire over both the creation of the universe and the progress of history: "The Lord by wisdom founded the earth; by understanding he established the heavens; by his knowledge the deeps broke forth, and the clouds drop down dew" (3, 19-20). "By me kings reign, and rulers decree what is just; by me princes rule, and nobles govern the earth" (8, 15-16).

If we are not too careful here, we can completely miss the point. Among all God's perfections, wisdom is the one that best explains his intervention in creation. When we read with more care, we see that our Wisdom exemplifies more than the perfection of a wonder-worker. She is the principle that presided over the elaboration of the cosmos. She is the principle, too, who placed every mortal in existence. Here we come upon one of the Bible's great truths: one and the same plan embraces *creation* and *human history*. The creative act is the first act of the great drama that terminates in the Redemption.

We should avoid too hasty a comparison of Israel's religion with the religion of the ancient orientals. These also admit of a strong bond uniting the religious destiny of a people to the act of creation. Like the most ancient biblical texts, Babylonian beliefs emphasized the relationship which at creation indissolubly joins the royalty of the national god and its external expressions, viz., investiture of the king, foundation of the temple, erection of the royal city. Since wisdom was looked upon as the king's virtue par excellence, it was logical to associate it with these different themes, as does a relatively recent text inserted in the Book of Jeremiah: "But the Lord is the true God. It is he who made the earth by his power, who established the world by his wisdom, and by his understanding stretched out the heavens" (Jer. 10, 10, 12).

However, the meaning the Bible gives this divine kingship is totally original. While other religions interpreted this kingship as the absolute dominion of the god over his land, each forming an indissoluble whole as old as the world itself, Israel had never believed that it was in virtue of an eternal right that Yahweh had set it in its territory. Israel realized fully that if it set foot in Palestine, it is at a precise moment of its history and through a decision of its God who had permitted it to chase out the original inhabitants. Yahweh, it is true, will become King there, but only after the country has been conquered.

It is elsewhere that we must seek the link that unites his kingship to creation. The latter prepares the coming of the former: the one is the prelude of an historical "event," while the other is its conclusion. Far from being the effect of a kind of necessity, this chain of events comes from the free will of God: Yahweh has as freely contracted an alliance with his people as he has drawn creation out of nothing. The same eternal thought which is at the origin of the universe and of history develops with unfailing continuity; but it does not allow itself to be subject to any law, even though it has conceived and established all law. The divine plan adapts itself to the reactions of a humanity that is rebellious and slow to understand. Everything takes place as though God, who embraces all history in one glances, never ceases retouching the changes in his own immutable plan.

No inspired writer has brought out the transcendence of the divine plan as well as Second Isaiah. He who says: "Who has performed and done this, calling the generations from the beginning? I, the Lord, the first, and with the last; I am he"

(Is. 41, 4), is the God who enfolds within his word everything coming into being in time: "The grass withers, the flower fades; but the word of God will stand for ever" (Is. 40, 8).

The introduction to Proverbs emphasizes the same idea. Though the ancient sages set the origin of their knowledge in the distant past, not one of them would pretend to place this origin beyond the limits of time itself. Israel's Wisdom, however, who presides at the destiny of the universe and the chosen people, lay claim to being anterior to all created things: "The Lord created me at the beginning of his work, the first of his acts of old. Ages ago I was set up, at the first, before the beginning of the earth. When there were no depths I was brought forth, when there were no springs abounding with water. Before the mountains had been shaped, before the hills, I was brought forth; before he had made the earth with its fields, or the first of the dust of the world. When he established the heavens I was there, when he drew a circle on the face of the deep, when he made firm the skies above, when he established the fountains of the deep, when he assigned to the sea its limits, so that the waters might not transgress his command, and when he marked out the foundations of the earth . . ." (8, 22-29).

With regard to the creation of Wisdom (cf. 8, 23), it is interesting to read the variants offered the exegetes. According to the Septuagint version, Wisdom was *established* from the beginning, as one would speak of the temple or the holy city being established. The Hebrew text says that Wisdom was *anointed* before all things, bringing to mind the idea of enthronement. The Theodotian version states that Wisdom was *formed* from all eternity, and in doing so it reminds us of the election of the god-king's son formed in the maternal womb. And since the image is feminine, it is reminiscent of the poem dedicated to the birth of Hatschepsout, daughter of Amon and sister-spouse of Toutemes II. We preferred the last variant. It sheds light concerning what the poet later on is to say concerning Wisdom's childhood: "Then I was beside him, like a little child and I was daily his delight, rejoicing before him always, rejoicing in his inhabited world and delighting in the sons of men" (8, 30-31). This young child is like Israel, the child for whom Yahweh was "as one who lifts an infant close against his cheek; stooping down to him I gave him his food" (Hos. 11, 4).

Wisdom, we have seen, lacks no title for laying claim to the new and authentic Israel. Is not the royal character, which she attributes to herself, that inheritance of the Davidic dynasty which Yahweh, through the voice of his prophet, transferred to the whole people (Is. 55, 3-4)? With this difference, however, that, although it would be inconceivable for a prince or a royal people to be anterior to creation, one could say this of Wisdom, that ideal Israel, who urged the historic Israel to adhere to and to incorporate itself into the eternal thought which it incarnated. In this Wisdom alone could the Elect and the Design that presided over the election coincide and intermingle.

* * *

If St. Paul will say of Christ, without being misunderstood, "He is before all things, and in him all things hold together" (Col. 1, 17), "even as he chose us in him before the foundation of the world" (Eph. 1, 4), it is because the notion of a Messiah antecedent to the created universe had been prepared for a long time by the notion that the world we were to enter transcended all existing realities. Does not the affirmation of the Word's divinity find for St. Athanasius its foundation in the consciousness of our own divinization: "If the Word is not God, then we are not divinized."

Christ himself, to support his claim to equality with the Father, will not hesitate to lean on that verse of the psalmist: "Have I not said, 'you are gods'?"

All this is found in germ in the famous page of Proverbs we

have quoted. In fact, what else does it say other than that we share in a mystery which surpasses all created things when we enter into the design of God?

The Incarnation of the Word will cast its light upon this in a very definite way, but we can meditate upon the meaning of this text in the Old Testament. It states that Wisdom was before creation. Everything is dependent upon her teaching and is subject to her activity. Placing his hand upon each of us, God makes us enter a new world which is not foreign to this world, but which surpasses it infinitely. The Elect is not withdrawn from his dwelling place, but he is no longer enclosed by it. He continues to move within it, but is no longer its slave.

Was not the Jew, preparing for the coming of the Messiah, already able to read in the hymn of Proverbs the statement of St. Paul: "All things are yours" (1 Cor. 3, 21-22). Everything is ours in Wisdom, for Wisdom belongs to God.

# THE BOOK OF JOB

2 The Book of Job, which is without analogue in the Scripture Canon, belongs to the *drama genre*.

According to the general opinion, the book is made up essentially of the complaint of Job, the discussion with his three friends, and the conclusion which introduces a new personage, Yahweh. He is to decide the debated question. This drama in verse is presented within the framework of a prologue and an epilogue, drawn from a popular story which gives rise to the drama. This story is touched up by the author and he blends it into his poem.

The result is a harmonious structure, an interior movement, and a simplicity of line that places the work in a class with the ancient Greek tragedies. If this unity has frequently been discussed or contested by the critics, it is because the text, as they admit, has undergone many a change and a touching up.

It seems impossible, in our opinion, to look upon the intervention of Elihu (32-37) as anything else but as interpolation.

Likewise, the eulogy of Wisdom (28) must be taken as an independent development, badly inserted in its context. With this reservation, however, that, corresponding with the thesis of the drama, it can very well have been from the same pen.

Finally, the third cycle of discourse (22-27) does not appear to us as having been transmitted in its original order: certain passages must be restored to other personages other than those to whom the text attributes them. A reconstruction being imperative, we have adopted that proposed by the excellent judgment of the Bible of Jerusalem.

The Book of Job must have been composed sometime after the Introduction to the Book of Proverbs, at a time when the memory of the Exile was very much alive, undoubtedly towards the middle of the fifth century.

### A.- THE SUFFERING OF A CHILD OF ISRAEL

The Book of Job is justly considered among the great masterpieces of all time. It is not simply a dissertation, such as a Cicero or a Seneca could have written, but it is the echo of a living experience. Its pathos cedes in no way to that described in the Promotheus of Aeschylus, the Oedipus of Sophocles, the Phaedra of Racine. These works have become immortal because they plumbed the depths of suffering which is humanity's chief characteristic. Job himself, as has often been said, is the mouthpiece of *universal suffering*. This is what brings him close to us, and it is the reason that he has won the submission of those least willing to admit the inspired character of his poem. Job belongs to all times and to all creeds.

But we would be reducing the importance and interest of its testimony if we were to recognize only the literary and philosophical value of the work. The experience he lived is not polyvalent. To understand it, one has only to enter more deeply into his suffering and, to do this, he has to get at the real cause.

\*  \*  \*

It is evident that the same trial affects in a totally different way the heart and mind of people who have not received the same background and formation. The horror of a concentration camp, for instance, does not have the same effect upon a "western" politician, a criminal, a priest, or the supporter of a dictator. In the same way, if a peasant of Upper Egypt had been able to know misfortunes as cruel as those of Job, his mournful and resigned distress would be lost in a silence which neither the noise of fortune nor the song of happiness had ever animated; Job's cry of pain, on the contrary, gives evidence of the sharp regret that swept over him at the ruin of his most marvelous dream.

Job's suffering is not well understood unless one can understand the suffering experienced by a son of Israel in the fifth century, after the ruin of the City and the Temple, and after the sad trials of Exile and the depressing experiences of the Return.

❊ ❊ ❊

Let us recall that these Hebrews were the ones whom Yahweh had delivered from slavery on the banks of the Nile. He had made them into a people and set them up in the land of Canaan. He had entered into a solemn Covenant with them, and his prophets and psalmists for centuries had opened up magnificent perspectives for them. Hence they jealously guarded in their heart, which was filled with hope, the dream which the promises of the God of Sinai justified. In the impatience of their long expectation their souls suffered in the extreme.

How, then, could such a people fail to undergo terrible anguish at the faintest appearance of anything contrary to this dream? We are not in Egypt where the same light bathes the joys and the griefs that come in that endless monotonous cycle of events.

Scarcely has Israel taken root in the promised land, like a

vine in rich soil, when it is torn up and driven away for its sins. And the Jews return from the Exile only to be soon dispersed throughout the world, everywhere wanderers and strangers, always haunted by the sharp desire of setting foot once again on that soil where they can feel themselves at home. In each there burns the flame of an inextinguishable nostalgia.

The Prologue presents Job to us as a semi-nomad, the brother of the patriarchs of Genesis, but just as his friends and the author, he does not think it possible to live outside the country formerly given to his people by Yahweh, that country in which: "rivers and streams flowed with honey and curds" (20, 17). "Its roots spread out to the waters, with the dew all night on its branches" (29, 19).

Bildad thus expresses himself in his definition of happiness: "He thrives before the sun, and his roots spread over the garden. His roots twine about the stone-heap; he lives among the rocks" (8, 16-17).

The eloquent image of the tree is found everywhere; man perished when, like the tree, he is uprooted: "If he is destroyed from his place, then it will deny him, saying, 'I have never seen you'" (8, 18). "His roots dry up beneath, and his branches wither above" (18, 16; cf. 15, 29-30).

The Middle Ages associated life with movement, and the Bible associates it with something solidly planted in the soil. The worst misfortune that can happen is to be uprooted: "The east wind lifts him up and he is gone; it sweeps him out of his place" (27, 21). "That they are like straw before the wind, and like chaff that the storm carries away" (21, 18).

There is nothing stable for the unfortunate, for his life drifts away like a piece of wreckage, carried by the waves: "My days are swifter than a runner; they flee away, they see no good. They go by like skiffs of reed, like an eagle swooping on the prey" (9, 25-26). His life vanishes away like a dream: "He will fly away like a dream, and not be found; he will be chased away like a vision of the night" (20, 8). There is no longer any room for hope: "My days are swifter than a weaver's shuttle, and come to their end without hope" (7, 6). "My days are past, my plans are broken off, the desires of my heart" (17, 11). Nothing belonging to the unfortunate man will remain, not even his memory through which he would have survived on earth: "His memory perishes from the earth, and he has no name in the street" (18, 17).

While the *panta rei* left the Greek philosopher indifferent, this *gliding towards death* freezes the Jew with fright, as if the experience of the Exile awakened in him the presentiment of the long and sorrowful *diaspora* which will come once the bond that united him to the soil has been broken: "The heavens will reveal his iniquity, and the earth will rise up against him" (20, 27). "If he is destroyed from his place, then it will deny him, saying, 'I have never seen you'" (8, 18). The law uses the very same threat with the guilty: "*You will be cut off from the country.*"

Peaceful possession of the land is Israel's dearest prayer. It was also its hope. Upon entering the land of Canaan, the Hebrews had no doubt of their permanent installation there, or that they would enjoy unchangeable peace, like a rock inaccessible to the fury of the waves. Had not David, the work of conquest completed, founded an hereditary kingdom and built his capital upon unshakable foundations?

The beautiful dream did not end there. In the euphoria of this seemingly endless establishment, the imagination was fired with the notion of *universal peace* in which all would be reconciled to each other. Though history inflicted a terrible awakening upon this dream, it did not impair hope but strengthened it. The dream was stimulated by trials in direct proportion to their oppressiveness. This contagious illusion is found both in Cophar and Job: "And you will have confidence, because there is hope;

you will be protected and take your rest in safety. You will lie down, and none will make you afraid; many will entreat your favor" (11, 18-19). "You shall not fear destruction when it comes. At destruction and famine you shall laugh, and shall not fear the beasts of the earth. For you shall be in league with the stones of the field, and the beasts of the field shall be at peace with you" (5, 21-23).

Job, however, is too well instructed by experience to be taken in by a dream which is only a dream in spite of its attractiveness. He has only to consider himself as living: "Man wastes away like a rotten thing, like a garment that is moth-eaten" (13, 28). God has only to withdraw for a moment: "They grope in the dark without light; and he makes them stagger like a drunken man" (12, 25).

Where then do man's hope and assurance lie? "Terrors are turned upon me; my honor is pursued as by the wind, and my property has passed away like a cloud" (30, 15). No obstacle opposes the assailant: "They break up my path, they promote my calamity; no one restrains them. As through a wide breach they come; amid the crash they roll on" (30, 13-14).

Vigilance is neither efficacious nor even possible: "He goes to bed rich, but will do so no more; he opens his eyes, and his wealth is gone. Terrors overtake him like a flood; in the night the whirlwind carries him off" (27, 19-20). "Terrifying sounds are in his ears; in prosperity the destroyer will come upon him" (15, 21). Having one's roots in the soil is no longer a pledge of security: "How much more those who dwell in houses of clay whose foundation is in the dust" (4, 19). "The house which (man) builds is like a spider's web" (27, 18). "He leans against his house, but it does not stand; he lays hold of it, but it does not endure" (8, 15). Everything is a snare for him; everything is adversity and the subject of anxiety. Everything seems to overthrow him; and his torment follows him even to his last refuge in sleep: "For the thing that I fear comes upon me, and what I dread befalls me. I am not at ease, nor am I quiet; I have no rest; but trouble comes" (3, 25-26).

If only there were some respite! But one trial follows upon another, and the messengers of evil came in quick succession, giving him no time to regain his composure: "While he was yet speaking, there came another and said . . ." (1, 16-18). If, like Israel, Job had not dreamed so much of peace and security, his disappointment would not have been so great and his confusion so poignant.

✿  ✿  ✿

However, in order to understand the secret of his sorrow, it is not enough to see the disenchantment consequent upon the shattered dream of a peaceful and prosperous possession of the land granted by Yahweh. Something else is cruelly wounded within him, the desire for action, that *insatiable love of life.*

Because of Israel's unyielding confidence in Yahweh's protection, it had never ceased probing into the future. Israel always felt that its destiny would open one day upon a limitless horizon. It is the people of hope par excellence. And this people was not content simply to dream about this, but it felt it necessary to throw itself into action with enthusiasm and passion. Its life had a definite meaning, and its journey had a definite goal. Both meaning and goal were mysterious and transcendent. So sure was Israel of this, it did not hesitate to sacrifice the present in order to hasten the future. Its deep-seated optimism was filled with eagerness.

Now before him Job claims there is nothing but a wall, and this wall is constructed by other than human hands: "He has walled up way, so that I cannot pass" (19, 8). Should he look out over the horizon? This would be folly as the space around him is diminishing more and more: "His strong steps are shortened and his own schemes throw him down. A trap seizes him by the heel, a snare lays hold of him" (18, 7-9).

How could Job walk when he did not know where to set his foot? His need for action is increased by the need for *light*: "Oh, that I were in the months of old, as in the days when God watched over me; when his lamp shone upon my head, and by his light I walked through darkness" (29, 2-3).

The sun's changes impregnated Egypt's whole life, and there was no people so taken up with the subject of light as the Greeks. This is true, but we feel that nowhere else was the theme of light the bearer of hope as it was in the land of Israel. Man awaits the dawn in Israel with the expectation of the psalmist's watchman (Ps. 130, 6), for light is the sign of the divine benevolence: "They make night into day; 'Thy light,' they say, 'is near to the darkness'" (17, 12). And will not the day of the Lord be as bright as light, and will not the failure to see its splendor be the greatest of misfortunes? The prophet threatens this for Israel's infidelity: "Why would you have the day of the Lord? It is darkness and not light" (Amos 5, 18). Is this, then, the curse that has befallen Job? "But when I looked for good, evil came; and when I waited for light, darkness came" (30, 26). It is like the night falling heavily upon the eyes of the dead: "and on my eyelids is deep darkness" (16, 16). "My eye has grown dim with grief" (17, 7).

This is the sudden fall into the darkness of chaos from which no one rises. The Bible refuses to reassure and console itself by feeding upon the illusion of an Osiric ascension toward the light of day. This is why Job seeks a moment of respite: "before I go when I shall not return, to the land of gloom and deep darkness, the land of gloom and chaos, where light is as darkness" (10, 21-22).

But what does it matter if this darkness has begun to swallow

him up? Even if he were to see as in clear daylight, what would
he see besides life's vanity, the failure of his efforts, the ruin of
his pride and joy, viz., health, success, riches, longevity and
prosperity? In short, he would be faced with the retreat from
the *shalom* promised the just man, whose steps God directs
and whose labors he blesses. "You shall know that your tent is
safe, and shall inspect your fold and miss nothing. You shall
know also that your descendants shall be many, and your offspring as the grass of the earth. You shall come to your grave
in ripe old age, as a shock of grain comes up to the thrashing
floor in its season" (5, 24-26).

Job cannot think of that *shalom* without bitter irony. It was
withdrawn from him who deserved it and bestowed upon the
wicked: "Their children are established in their presence, and
their offspring before their eyes. Their houses are safe from
fear, and no rod of God is upon them. Their bull breeds without
fail; their cow calves, and does not cast her calf. They send
forth their little ones like a flock, and their children dance. They
sing to the tambourine and the lyre, and rejoice to the sound
of the pipe. They spend their days in prosperity, and in peace
they go down to Sheol" (21, 8-13).

Why doubt and despair of everything? The heart of an
Israelite is impatient to advance, but he must believe in happiness
in order to start out on the journey. Job was not unaware of
this, but he was dissipated like smoke.

The man in affliction, unless he seeks out some illusory refuge
in the past, remains nailed to the spot and is eaten up by a
dynamism that has no object. And Job does not resist undertaking
the vainest and saddest of journeys, viz., that of his memories.
When he looks back what a luxuriant strength filled his life!
"One dies in full properity, being wholly at ease and secure,
his body full of fat and the marrow of his bones moist"
(21, 23-24).

How he used to see the evening of a long day coming on gently, haloed with honor and respect! "Then I thought, 'I shall die in my nest, and I shall multiply my days as the sand'" (29, 18).

*   *   *

Memories, however, are vain! His dead eyes are turned toward the future. Job is but weakness, bound up by humiliation and sickness and misery. This desire for life and action, inherent in his race, does not want to die. To satisfy itself, it has nothing but cries of rebellion. How can one resign himself to believing that life has no meaning? that conduct, constantly guided by the commandments of God and the Covenant, does not receive its reward in the fullness of being? Yet how can one deny what is? And how can one fail to be torn by this frightful and incomprehensible contradiction?

Such suffering might not have been any better understood by the Egyptian of the Empire than by the Moslem. The first, when he complained, could think of nothing but the boredom of life; as for the second, never was his existence lighted up by any messianic hope. Job himself, if he suffers, it is because he feels that his devouring dynamism is condemned to stir up nothing but the void; his suffering is also like one who has been awakened from a dream which suddenly appears to have been too beautiful and too great. His disappointment will be just as bitter as his hopes have been vast. And within the depths of Job's heart it is the heart of Israel that is beating: no people has suffered as much as Israel, because no people ever expected so much from God.

B.- GOD'S SILENCE

Just as the suffering of Job is not a simple echo of universal suffering, so the drama in which it is expressed does not claim to pose a problem of theodicy. Regarding the first point, we have shown that Job's torment is none other than that of the son of Israel who, in his impatience, had expected too much from the Covenant. On the second point, in spite of the long discussion that fills it, what the drama gives us is a lived experience — perhaps the most pathetic of spiritual experiences: and it is this that we now propose to show and explain.

*　*　*

Job begins with evidence that his friends vainly try to deny. Far from being crushed as it so richly deserves, *injustice* triumphs upon the earth with great insolence: "Men remove landmarks; they seize flocks and pasture them" (24, 2). "Who declares his way to his face, and who requites him for what he has done? When he is borne to the grave, watch is kept over his tomb. The clods of the valley are sweet to him; all men following after him, and those who go before him are innumerable" (21, 31-33).

On the other hand, poor people, having no support but their own innocence and good will, are dispossessed of their goods and their dignity: "They drive away the ass of the fatherless; they take the widow's ox for a pledge. They thrust the poor off the road; the poor of the earth all hide themselves" (24, 3-4). When not forced to withdraw, they are drawn into a mercenary, uncertain, and sad life: "They gather the fodder in the field and they glean the vineyard of the wicked man. They go about naked without clothing; hungry, they carry the sheaves" (24, 6, 10).

This twofold injustice is an aggravating enigma for Job: "Why do the wicked live, reach old age, and grow mighty in power?" (21, 7). His life is filled with anguish because the question goes unanswered: "When I think of it I am dismayed, and shuddering seizes my flesh" (21, 6). How can one ignore the incomprehensible scandal? Must one but speak sophisms, saying: "that the wicked man is spared in the day of calamity, that he is rescued in the day of wrath"? (21, 30). Job cannot accept the traditional arguments which his friends constantly din in his ears. These arguments substantiate teachings already accepted, but he finds them useless: "Your maxims are proverbs of ashes, your defenses are defenses of clay" (13, 12). Rather than deny actuality, it is better to call the creator into question: "When disaster brings sudden death, he mocks at the calamity of the innocent. The earth is given into the hand of the wicked; he covers the faces of the judges, if it is not he, who then is it? (9, 23-24). Does this mean, as his friends imply, that he is reproaching God for being blind, incapable of preventing or punishing crime? Will he sneeringly say as did the impious of the past "What does God know? Can he judge through the deep darkness?" (22, 13-14). Job is not an impious man, nor has he thus spoken. Though he comes in conflict with the inexplicable, he contests in no way God's position as supreme Judge. In spite of his words, he needs only recall the sigh following his proud and passionate pleading to convince himself of his faith in the divine sanctions: "For I was in terror of calamity from God, and I could not have faced his majesty" (31, 23).

True, he betrays here his faith in Yahweh's power rather than in his justice. But does he not summon his friends before the Most High's tribunal, because they have nothing but the distributive justice of God on their lips? If Job believes in Yahweh's justice, it is because this justice is in the reasonableness of the divine work. For example, the wicked, trusting in the freedom from punishment they are now experiencing, have vainly believed the heavens are empty and cry out: "No eye will see us!" (24, 15). But they will escape neither remorse nor anguish: "For deep darkness is morning to all of them; for they are friends with the terrors of deep darkness" (24, 17).

Evil is identified with darkness, whether it is chastised or not. Wrapped in the shadows of the night, the assassin lies in wait, the thief does his prowling, and the adulterer steals to his illicit lover: "The murderer rises in the dark, that he may kill the poor and needy; and in the night he is as a thief. The eye of the adulterer also waits for the twilight" (24, 14-15).

This association of crime with darkness is no mere literary comparison. From the beginning evil was routed by the appearance of light, and from the midst of the tempest Yahweh will remind Job: "Have you commanded the morning since your days began, and caused the dawn to know its place, that it might take hold of the skirts of the earth, and the wicked to be shaken out of it? From the wicked their light is withheld, and their uplifted arm is broken" (38, 12-13, 15).

God pierces through the pride of the wicked whenever he wills, just as his conquering arm subdues the mythical Behemoth and Leviathan. When suggesting ironically that Job take his place, Yahweh describes himself as the Judge capable of handling things: "Deck yourself with majesty and dignity; clothe yourself with glory and splendor. Pour forth the overflowings of your anger, and look on every one that is proud, and abase him. Look on every one that is proud, and bring him low; and tread down the wicked where they stand. Hide them all in the dust together; bind their faces in the world below" (40, 10-13).

Job never doubted that every intervention of God in the history of men was only a manifestation of his justice.

* * *

Job's faith and experience seem to stand in contradiction of each other. Stating that innocence is overcome and injustice triumphs, Job calls into doubt the direction of creation; his friends do not fail to point this out. In reality, if he complains, it is not because he doubts divine power and justice but that they are not being exercised: "Why are not times of judgment kept by the Almighty, and why do those who know him never see his days?" (24, 1).

Yes, what upsets him in this contradiction is that Yahweh is silent, that he *"hides his face,"* that upon creation lies an unbearable quiet, and man can only say: "I cry to thee and thou dost not answer me!" (30, 20).

Why this silence? Is not Job the creature lovingly formed in the womb by the divine hand? "Remember that thou hast made me of clay; and wilt thou turn me to dust again? Thou didst clothe me with skin and flesh, and knit me together with bones and sinews. Thou hast granted me life and steadfast love; and thy care preserved my spirit" (10, 9-12).

And this creature is not any creature whatsoever, but one upon whom Yahweh has placed his hand, one who because of his docility can trust in him: "although thou knowest that I am not guilty, and there is none to deliver me out of thy hand" (10, 7).

❖ ❖ ❖

Coming upon the idea once again of the Election, how can we fail to be struck by the apparent connection between Job's experience and that of Israel, and of the Israel of the dark centuries following the Exile?

What holds for the People as a whole holds for each of its members. What the prophets said to Israel, the sages say to each individual. Now, sages and prophets think, speak, and act only in relationship to the *Covenant.* We might say of the sage and the prophet: "What wise men have told, and their fathers have not hidden, to whom alone the land is given, and no stranger passed among them" (15, 18-19).

Like Job, Israel is the *"suffering just one"* par excellence. In the past, Yahweh frequently had to force his people to respect the conditions of the Covenant, and these corrections were those of a father as rich in mercy as he was swift in anger: "Behold, happy is the man whom God reproves; therefore, despise not the chastening of the Almighty. For he wounds, but he binds up; he smites, but his hands heal" (5, 17-18).

But there is question now of a new Israel seeking itself, and it will not be long in finding itself.

Those who pursue the ideal of innocence and justice, incarnated in the new Israel, appear as the ones most disinherited; they are the ones most oppressed by the powerful and whom hated attacks most violently. Why does the trial never let up? Why do they alone on earth not experience the joy of success?

When God chastised its sins, Israel had no complaint to make. But when it was obedient, how was it to resign itself when foreign nations triumphed, and when the honor of the divine name demanded that in their turn they too should drink the chalice of the divine anger? Did not the prophets at the time of Israel's infidelity, denouncing the ephemeral character of their victories, fulminate oracles of death against its enemies as though they would have lost face in the eyes of all? And is it not now that God's justice should intervene? If under the breath of the Almighty the impious do not finally disappear, what is really the meaning of the Election of Israel?

In the same way, the inexplicable lot of Job presents, in the face of the immunity accorded to the wicked, an enigma which demands God's intervention not only because of the demands of divine justice but also because of those of the Election.

*    *    *

In either case God's silence runs the risk of rendering the Election meaningless. Israel, as long as it was able to believe in its extraordinary destiny, tried to live up to its dream with enthusiastic fervor: "Is not your fear of God your confidence?" (4, 6). Even the most serious trials did not dampen its faith, for were these not merited corrections? "For affliction does not come from the dust, nor does trouble sprout from the ground" (5, 6).

Man, the artisan of his evils, can also be the artisan of his healing. To walk in Yahweh's paths it is sufficient to will it and *be converted*: "If you set your heart aright, you will stretch out your hands towards him. If iniquity is in your hand, put it far away, and let not wickedness dwell in your tents" (11, 13-14). Trial would thus be only a passing thing which is quickly forgotten: "You will forget your misery; you will remember it as the waters that have passed away" (11, 16). "And though your beginning was small, your latter days will be very great" (8, 7).

Though in the same destiny the just and the unjust intermingle: "Yahweh destroys the blameless and the wicked" (9, 22), everything becomes uncertain for the man for whom there remains nothing more than to cry out like Job: "I am blameless; I regard not myself; I loathe my life" (9, 21), and give himself up to despair: "I become afraid of all my suffering, for I know thou wilt not hold me innocent. I shall be condemned; why then do I labor in vain? If I wash myself with snow, and cleanse my hands with lye, yet thou wilt plunge me into a pit, and my own clothes will abhor me" (9, 28-31).

Man is reached in his living powers. Before him there stretches out a deserted and hostile road. His life is no longer worth the trouble of being lived. "I loathe my life; I will give free utterance to my complaint" (10, 1). "When I lie down I say, 'When shall I arise?' But the night is long, and I am full of tossing till the dawn" (7, 4).

What is the use, then, of living, hoping, and struggling? "Why is light given to him that is in misery, and life to the bitter in soul, who longs for death, but it comes not, and digs for it more than for hid treasures; who rejoice exceedingly, and are glad, when they find the grave? Why is light given to man whose way is hid, whom God has hedged in?" (3, 20-23).

Is it not better to abandon oneself without resistance and fall

into Sheol? The unfortunate one will at least be in his own place;
"If I say to the pit, 'You are my father,' and to the worm, 'My
mother,' or 'My sister'" (17, 14).

As for existence, there is nothing more to do than give it over
to the enemies of creation and to the ancient monsters of the
deep. Let everything fall back into chaos. Let the child of man
never again see the light of day, for he is condemned in advance
to sharing an insufferable destiny. "Why did thou bring me forth
from the womb?" (10, 18).

*    *    *

If one could imagine a life beyond this one and if there was
a refuge of hope, things would not be so bad.

We ask ourselves, at times, why the author of Job did not
draw from the Egyptians' belief in a future life. His sufferings
then would have some meaning. But, unless we are unaware of
the true perspectives of the ancient religions and falsify them
by observing them through the prism of modern thought and
then Christian thought, we cannot ask such a question.

Job was unable, without denying the spirit of Moses' teaching,
to dream of such a "contamination." Never did ancient Egypt
conceive of an after-life in which our earthly course would come
to an end and in which it would receive reward or punishment.
The dead one was simply admitted to following the nocturnal
periplus of Osiris. Osiris is simply the reverse side of Horus, his
son, who springs each morning from the maternal womb; Horus
is the true living one. Such a belief was incompatible with the
teaching of Israel which, liberated from the cyclic rhythm to
which the ancient religions had remained prisoners, had long
since learned from Yahweh the total *irreversibility of its destiny*:
"For there is hope for the tree, if it be cut down, that it will
sprout again, and that its shoots will not cease. . . . But man dies,
and is laid low; man breathes his last, and where is he? . . . so
man lies down and rises not again; till the heavens are no more

he will not awake, or be roused out of his sleep" (14, 7, 10, 12).

It appears that defeat is irremediable. Job has shown this to us better than he has revealed his sores. This is part of the Covenant. In the divine work a gap appears which no effort of the imagination is able to fill. The God of justice and love who has chosen Israel remains silent; and his silence is impenetrable. It remains his secret, and he alone is able to reveal the meaning of his intervention into the history of men and to open new horizons for his chosen ones, giving them a renewed desire to live. It will then be revealed that this world's realities lie beyond time, and it is there that Wisdom leads them.

God's answer, though close at hand, did not reach Job. For the moment, with Israel, he contemplates in bewilderment an abyss which the optimism of Israel's prophets and its first sages had not allowed him to even suspect.

C.- THE HAND OF GOD

Israel sees the hopes it had placed in Yahweh disappear; Job is filled with anguish at the apparent vanity of a destiny that has no explanation. Is Yahweh forgetting his Elect? Job and Israel can easily believe this. But is it possible that the torment of the searching heart and the confusion of the doubting soul are the advance signs of discovery? Yahweh is silent, true; but silence is not absence. Israel and Job fully realize this. So possessive is this presence, that neither Israel nor Job would forget he is under the hand of God.

✲   ✲   ✲

It is time now to show how much Job's ideas differ from those of his friends with regard to this providence of God.

A too hasty reading of the drama could render this doubtful: theories rather than men appear to be brought face to face in the drama. In each person there is the same argument, sustained by the same lyricism; throughout the work, we find the same magnificent evocation of the divine omnipotence. This is so true that many of the passages were able to be ascribed indifferently to anyone of the interlocutors; the exegetes, therefore, experience some trouble in reconstructing the third cycle of the discourses. To guide them there is the position taken by each personage regarding the theory of retribution.

But is this the only thing separating Job from his friends? With a little attention, it soon becomes evident he and they speak differently about God.

Eliphaz, Bildad, and Cophar, in their dissertation on human suffering and on the order of the world, seem to see nothing beyond man and his condition. While boasting of upholding the divine justice, it happens that they evoke the chastisement of the wicked without once pronouncing the divine name. In stating Yahweh's role as Judge, they reduce him to the role of executing only their own conception of justice. To them, God is limited in sanctioning in some automatic way merits and demerits. Each one remains the master of his own destiny since innocence engenders happiness as rigorously as injustice engenders misfortune. Hence, to escape the latter, all a man must do is become wise: "You will be delivered through the cleanness of your hands" (22, 30).

This is totally an edifice built on reason, in which the supreme Judge is the keystone insuring its stability rather than one whose power sustains the Elect in love. Old Eliphaz will say: "Can a man be profitable to God? Surely he who is wise is profitable to himself. Is it any pleasure to the Almighty if you are righteous, or is it gain to him if you make your ways blameless?" (12, 2-3). He speaks as though there was no interest in Israel's conduct on Yahweh's part, or as though his honor and glory were not linked with the destiny of the people whom he had chosen. It seems here that only a step separates the God of the Bible from the God of the philosophers; and only a step has to be taken to create a concept of the divinity from which Marxism will one day want to liberate humanity.

Job, on the contrary, centers all his attention on God. The sole term of his meditations or his complaints, Yahweh, far from being simply the first cause of the universe upon whom falls the care of divine justice, is first and foremost the living God of Sinai. He is the God who, in the most unforeseeable of initiatives, has set his hand upon Israel and who will never again permit his grasp to loosen. And it is this grasp to which Job bears witness throughout the entire poem. He does not expound, he lives; there are no arguments, there is an *experience*: "I was at ease, and he broke me asunder; he seized me by the neck and dashed me to pieces" (16, 12). "With violence it seizes my garments; it binds me about like the collar of my tunic" (30, 18).

For it is really a concrete, powerful, and full experience: "And if I lift myself up, thou dost hunt me like a lion" (10, 16). "Thou liftest me up on the wind, thou makest me ride on it, and thou tossest me about in the roar of the storm" (30, 22). "God has cast me into the mire, and I have become like dust and ashes" (30, 19).

We are reminded of Saul on the road to Damascus and of so many other men whom an *irresistible divine intrusion* laid hold of, snatching them from an easy way opened up before them and with which they were so content. God does not impose himself upon man without doing him violence. Here, however, the violence is so brutal that Yahweh seems to be furious: "He runs upon me like a warrior" (16, 14). "For the arrows of the Almighty are in me; my spirit drinks their poison" (6, 4). "Why hast thou made me thy mark?" (7, 20). "He slashes open my kidneys, and does not care" (16, 13). "Thou dost renew thy witnesses against me, and increase my vexations towards me; thou dost bring fresh hosts against me" (10, 17).

It is an unequal struggle in which Job is mercilessly tracked down. Never and in no place does the glance of Yahweh cease to weigh upon him: "How long wilt thou not look away from me, nor let me alone till I swallow my spittle?" (7, 19). "Am I the sea, or a sea monster, that thou settest a guard over me?" (7, 12).

Yahweh seems to grip his Elect as Phaedra will be grasped by the Greek goddess: "It is Venus attached to her prey."

Never before, in the Bible, has the divine control been so intensely described. Elsewhere, Israel shudders under the merciless hand that crushes it, but it has only itself to blame as it is a *stiff-necked* people. Here, what makes Yahweh's pursuit so startling is the fact that Job never made the attempt to withdraw from him. All through his life he had tried to keep the commandments; and he takes legitimate pride in doing so: "This would be my consolation; I would even exult in pain unsparing; for I have not denied the words of the Holy One" (6, 10).

Why, then, this pitiless pursuit? When Yahweh constrains Israel to re-enter his pasture because it has wandered away, it is through a movement of love that he does so. But to realize his mysterious design in spite of the hardness of his People, he has much time since he is master of the ages. In regard to one individual, is it the same? The divine action is limited by the brevity of human life: "Remember that my life is a breath" (7, 7).

Are such display of power and such animosity necessary to reach man? Does man merit such strict and pressing surveillance? "What is man, that thou dost make so much of him, and that thou dost set thy mind upon him?" (7, 17). "Wilt thou frighten a driven leaf and pursue dry chaff?" (8, 25).

Perhaps the Creator, "changing his mind" (10, 8), wills the destruction of his creature. "Yea, I know that thou will bring me to death, and to the house appointed for all living" (30, 23).

Hence, why does he not turn away his glance in order to allow his creature to die peacefully (14, 6), rather than torment his life which is nothing to him? "Thou prevailest forever against him, and he passes; thou changest his countenance, and sendest him away" (14, 20).

God cannot, however, be content with so passing a possession of his creature; and Job has a confused intuition of this. Would death withdraw his victims from him forever? "While thy eyes are upon me, I shall be gone" (7, 8). "Now I shall lie in the earth; thou shalt seek me, but I shall not be" (7, 21).

Though, not understanding why, Job has provoked Yahweh's anger, he knows this will be followed by mercy. So little is he in doubt about this that he dreams of a refuge where hidden he can await the return of grace: "Oh, that thou wouldst hide me in Sheol, that thou wouldst conceal me until thy wrath is past, that thou wouldst appoint me a set time, and remember me? If a man die, shall he live again? All the days of my service I would wait, till my release should come. Thou wouldst call, and I would answer thee; thou wouldst long for the work of thy hands" (14, 13-15).

❋   ❋   ❋

There is only one possible solution to this endless pursuit, a new encounter with Yahweh who will dispel in a decisive way the obscurities about which men debate. This is what Job longs for in his complaints. Although Yahweh, the sovereign ruler of time, can sacrifice a generation to conquer better succeeding generations of Israel, such conduct is inconceivable when it comes to one single man.

Death, once again, rises up for Job as an insoluble problem. The hour has not yet come when the necessity of a future life will be made clear, demanded not only by a justice (which in our experience is never exercised on earth) but especially by the Election. Unless it is totally empty of any meaning, this Election cannot fail to lead to its perfection the union of

Yahweh with his People. For the God of Abraham, Isaac, and Jacob is not the God of the dead but of the living.

### D.- THE JUDGMENT OF GOD ON THE WORLD

Yahweh asks Satan, "Have you considered my servant Job?" (1, 8).

The honest and upright Job fears God and avoids evil; better still, in sudden misfortune he *still holds fast to his integrity* (2, 3). Job makes God the center of his life and never ceases doing so. He is also the one who speaks the most correctly about God, even in the midst of his most vehement complaints. He will be the cause of drawing down God's mercy on Eliphaz, on Bildad and on Cophar, so sure of themselves as being God's mouthpiece. "Offer up for yourselves a burnt offering; and my servant Job shall pray for you, for I will accept his prayer not to deal with you according to your folly; for you have not spoken of me what is right, as my servant Job has" (42, 8).

Job certainly is the servant of Yahweh. But is he not really the incarnation of the whole religious destiny of the Jewish people? True, the patriarch originated in Uz, in the land of Edom, and the legend must be dated before the Sinai Covenant. But we must also take into account that, without denying the unique character of its vocation, Israel is constantly preoccupied with making its own particular case enter into a more general framework, viz., God's plan for the whole world. Israel's destiny is written into an economy of salvation in which all the patriarchs are involved before and after the Flood. Job is set up as a witness of what will later on be the condition of the Jew in the midst of all the nations.

✿    ✿    ✿

In fact, the drama of Job is not only that of the sufferings Yahweh appears to inflict on his Elect but also that of the judgment upon the Elect by the world. We may say, then, that through the mouth of Job's three friends, we have Israel's enemies who accuse it.

Israel always felt that the surrounding peoples were interested in its history. In the vividness of the events, these people were always able to see what Yahweh was able to do and actually willed to do for humanity. Also, Israel did not allow itself to take notice of their opinion. Though it rejoiced in the days of its glory over the discomfiture of foreign kings, it was exasperated, upon the advent of evil days by the evil interpretation placed on its trials by the stranger: "He was despised and rejected by men; a man of sorrow and acquainted with grief; and as one from whom men hide their faces, he was despised and we esteemed him not" (Is. 53, 3).

Could the stranger judge justly? How could a destiny so filled with contradictions, so often unintelligible to Israel itself, be correctly appreciated from the "outside"? God alone could explain its secret meaning. As long as he remained silent, his Elect could not be understood by the rest of the world, not even by its friends.

We must not be surprised then by the *solitude* to which the unfortunate one is relegated, for is this not a servitude consonant with the Election? The prophets, among them Jeremiah, experienced this in reality: "I sat alone because thy hand was upon me" (Jer. 15, 17).

We, too, withdraw instinctively from Job. Man has a presentiment of mystery, filling him with fright when he beholds misfortune. It is as though, the unfortunate one, a sign of the divine curse, threatened him with his own contagion: "They abhor me, they keep aloof from me" (30, 10). "He has put my brethren far from me, and my acquaintances are wholly estranged from me. My kinsfolk and my close friends have failed me; the guests in my house have forgotten me; my maidservants count me as a stranger; I have become an alien in their eyes. I call to my servant, but he gives me no answer; I must beseech him with my mouth. I am repulsive to my wife, loathsome to the sons of my own mother. Even young children despise me; when I rise they talk against me. All my intimate friends abhor me, and those whom I loved have turned against me" (19, 13-19).

They don't simply flee from Job. In order to separate themselves even more from the unfortunate one, they go so far as to heap insults and *outrages* upon him: "He has made me a byword of peoples, and I am one before whom men spit" (17, 6).

Has not the *"Vae victis"* of the Barbarian resounded throughout history from the tragedy of Calvary to the atrocities of the concentration camp? "In the thought of one who is at ease there is contempt for misfortune; it is ready for those whose feet slip" (12, 5).

Finally, they experience the necessity of justifying God's apparent condemnation in their own eyes. Their conscience will know no rest till they can say "Well done!" A narrow minded theology renders the service of self-assurance in the presence of the patriarch's misfortune.

They make the suggestion that he repent for the evil he has done. Undoubtedly, he has all the outward marks of holiness; but God's demands are great. Besides, who can lay any claim to innocence in God's presence? Then, irritated by Job's resistance which belittles their wisdom (an admission of guilt would so simplify matters!), they accuse him ruthlessly of all manner of crimes: "For you have exacted pledges of your brothers for nothing, and stripped the naked of their clothing. You have given no water to the weary to drink, and you have withheld bread from the hungry. The man with power possessed the land, and the favored man dwelt in it. You have sent widows away empty, and the arms of the fatherless were crushed" (22, 6-9).

Why this outburst of calumnies? Far from desiring to help the man *"lying in the ashes"* with their advice, they are thinking of nothing else but of self-reassurance by safeguarding the traditional view of things. "Therefore snares are round about you, and sudden terror overwhelms you" (22, 10).

Job cannot depend on them. He will have to continue all alone the great interior debate which gnaws away at him more cruelly than the reversal of his fortune, the ruins of his home, and the ulcers of his body.

"My brethren are treacherous as a torrent-bed, as freshets that pass away, which are dark with ice, and where the snow hides itself. In time of heat they disappear; when it is hot, they vanish from their place. The caravans of Tema look, the travelers of Sheba hope. They are disappointed because they were confident; they come hither and are confounded. Such you have now become to me; you see my calamity, and are afraid" (6, 15-21).

How has he failed in friendship himself? He has struck no blow at their goods, he has not exposed their life in his own defense (6, 22-23). Cowardice prevents a man from declaring in favor of the vanquished. The groans of suffering leave him insensible as long as these sufferings do not involve him: "Have pity on me, have pity on me, O you, my friends" (19, 21).

True, Job himself, when evoking the origin of his evils, urges them to be prudent and reserved: "... for the hand of God has touched me! Why do you, like God, pursue me? Know then that God has put me in the wrong, and closed his net about me" (19, 21-22, 6).

An admission of this kind should have awakened compassion in the three friends, but it alienates them from Job. They are hardened in their reproof of him because of their fear in the presence of the "sacred." Job sadly admits this: "I am a laughing-stock to my friends; I, who called upon God, and he answered me..." (12, 4).

Must one expect men of this calibre to place themselves between Yahweh and Job? "There is no umpire between us, who may lay his hand upon us both. Let him take away his rod from me, and let not the dread of him terrify me" (9, 33-34).

They feel it less dangerous if they turn out to be bad advocates, not of the most just, but of the strongest. However: "Will you show partiality towards him, will you plead the case for God? Will it be well with you when he searches you out? Or can you deceive him, as one deceives a man? He will surely rebuke you if in secret you show partiality" (8, 7-10).

*   *   *

An easy solution for Job's friends, and an easy one for him too, would simply be to bow his head under these accusations. Had he been able to create in himself some sort of guilt, it would have been perhaps some solace: the abdication would have furnished him a subtle means of stealing away from the presence of God, the presence which oppresses him. But, through fidelity to his faith, he refuses to stiffle the testimony of his conscience: "As long as my breath is in me, and the spirit of God is in my nostrils, my lips will not speak falsehood, and my tongue will not utter conceit. Far be it from me to say that you are right; till I die I will not put integrity from me. I hold fast my righteousness, and I will not let go" (27, 3-6).

Never will Job stoop to accept man's verdict. He will appeal to Yahweh alone to learn the cause of his grief. "But I would speak with the Almighty, and I desire to argue my case with God. As for you, you whitewash with lies; worthless physicians are you all" (8, 3-4).

On the verge of appealing to the Judge, he hesitates: "Though I am innocent I cannot answer him; I must appeal for mercy to my accuser" (9, 15).

Yahweh has always reserved to himself the initiative of the dialogue to which he has invited man. As he sees without being seen, so he speaks without being taken. It is folly for the creature to try to cross the unfathomable abyss separating him from infinite Transcendence. "Oh, that I knew where I could find him, that I might come even to his seat! I would lay my case before him and fill my mouth with arguments. . . . Behold, I go forward, but he is not there; and backward, but I cannot perceive him; on the left hand I seek him, but I cannot behold him; I turn to the right hand, but I cannot see him. . . . For I am hemmed in by darkness, and thick darkness covers my face" (23, 3-4, 8-9, 17).

Job makes up his mind fearfully, for innocent in his own eyes, what value will his plea have in Yahweh's eyes? "Though I am innocent, my mouth would condemn me; though I am blameless, he would prove me perverse" (9, 20).

Will the God of Sinai, who forced himself upon the Hebrews in the violence of the storm, answer the summons of a man? "For he is not a man as I am, that I might answer him, that we should come to trial together" (9, 32).

Mastering his terror, or as the text expresses it: "taking his flesh in his teeth," he dares confront him whom no one has seen without dying. He can do nothing else. "Behold he will slay me; I have no hope; yet I will defend my ways to his face" (13, 15).

Then he makes his confession (31, 5, 34), unsure of even being heard: "O that I had one to hear me!" (31, 35). At least he has raised his cry to God: "Here is my signature! let the Almighty answer me!" (31, 35).

If Yahweh will only listen then Job will be confident in his just cause. He is so sure of having refuted the accusations made against him that he cries out: "Oh, that I had the indictment written by my adversary! Surely I would carry it on my shoulder; I would bind it on me as a crown; I would give him an account of all my steps; like a prince I would approach him" (31, 35-37).

We might ask ourselves whether Job would have been better advised to be silent and not expose himself as God's equal, risking such a confrontation with the Almighty. He would then enjoy the grandeur of dying with sealed lips, strong in an innocence — far more eloquent than words.

Job could not allow the world to believe or to claim that he had failed in fidelity. He wants to denounce man's mistaken judgment with great protestations. There was no question of his living out a strictly personal experience but of his being God's witness and of being this in the presence of all.

Hence that strong cry in order to give an answer to all interpretations: "Oh, earth, cover not my blood, and let my cry find no resting place" (16, 18). "Oh, that my words were written! Oh, that they were inscribed in a book! Oh, that with an iron pen and lead they were graven in the rock forever" (19, 23-24).

Israel's trial since its return from the Exile is not due, as in the time of the kings, to its infidelities. And, in spite of all its claims, the world does not have the secret of the mystery any more than does Israel. Job is well aware of this, and he desires to see a solution to the terrible enigma under which he is crushed. "For I know that my Redeemer lives, and at last he will stand upon the earth" (19, 25).

E.- YAHWEH MAKES HIS APPEARANCE

Neither the elect who justifies himself nor the world who condemns him is able to penetrate the meaning of the mystery. The sole master of the secret is the one who remains silent, but of whom each is conscious in his own way. As the drama draws to its conclusion, the expectation of Yahweh's manifestation becomes more and more laden with anxiety.

And then there resounds the Voice which is more necessary for man than the very air he breathes. Will Yahweh be the one his antagonists imagined him to be?

Job's friends had represented him as the sovereign Judge of infallible pronouncements. One cannot believe otherwise, but it remains to be seen when and where he exercises this justice. Must we admit with Eliphaz and his companions that this justice enters into all circumstances and on the temporal plane? Apparently not, since even Yahweh challenges these imprudent advocates: "After the Lord had spoken these words to Job, the Lord said to Eliphaz the Temanite: 'My wrath is kindled against you and against your two friends; for you have not spoken of me, as my servant Job has'" (42, 7).

However, in spite of their excesses which so cruelly wounded Job, and in spite of the shortcomings of their teaching on retribution, their considerations of the divine work appear much more edifying than the wild cries of the holy man. One is frequently wrong, and to prove this it would be easy to cite translators, glossarists, and both old and new commentators. Against them there is the verdict of Yahweh already quoted: the three friends are severely judged, while Job alone is justified.

This justification, of course, · is totally relative: though Job wins the fight in the eyes of men, he can be convinced that his defense in the light of the divine Presence is inconsistent. He admits this with a humility that is in singular contrast with the pride of his plea: " 'Who is this that hides counsel without knowledge?' Therefore I have uttered what I did not understand, things too wonderful for me, which I did not know. 'Hear, and I will speak; I will question you, and you declare to me.' I had heard of thee by the hearing of the ear, but now my eye sees thee; therefore I despise myself, and repent in dust and ashes"

In this book we perceive three concepts of the divinity: that of Eliphaz, Bildad and Cophar; that of Job's experience; and finally the one revealed by God about himself.

*  *  *

Job's friends seem to speak of God as did the prophets. They give him honor as the God who assures salvation to all, without respect of the great of this world, nor neglect of the interests of the lowly and the disinherited. This is the God depicted in Second Isaiah, the one who raised up his humiliated Servant and set him before dumbfounded kings: "He sets on high those who are lowly, and those who mourn are lifted to safety. He frustrates the devices of the crafty, so that their hands achieve no success. He takes the wise in their own craftiness; and the schemes of the wily are brought to a quick end. They meet with darkness in the daytime, and grope at noonday as in the night. But he saves the fatherless from their mouth, the needy from the hand of the mighty. So the poor have hope, and injustice shuts her mouth" (5, 11-16).

Their God is the breaker of tyrants and impious men: "He hath pulled down the strong by his might..." (24, 22). "For he hath stretched out his hand against God, and bids defiance to the Almighty.... Let him not trust in emptiness, deceiving himself; for emptiness will be his recompense" (15, 25, 31).

He is the one also who protects the humble and crushes the proud: "For God abuses the proud, but he saves the lowly" (22, 29).

This perfect justice stems from the fact that he sits above the universe: "Is not God high in the heavens? See the highest stars, how lofty they are" (22, 12).

His sovereign presence, since it is independent of everything, envelopes everything: "Can you find out the deep things of God? Can you find out the limit of the Almighty? It is higher than heaven — what can you do? Deeper than Sheol — what can you know? Its measure is longer than the earth, and broader than the sea. If he passes through and imprisons, and calls to judgment, who can hinder him?" (11, 7-10).

Not only is he almighty, but his wisdom makes awesome demands. Divine holiness, whose herald Isaiah was, will insure Israel's triumph over all the nations some day, but it will make Israel conscious of its own sins and the need of total purification. Job's friends will repeat over and over again: "Can mortal man be righteous before God? Can a man be pure before his Maker? Even in her servants he puts no trust, and his angels he charges with error" (4, 17-18). "How can man be righteous before God? How can he who was born of woman be clean? Behold, even the moon is not bright and the stars are not clean in his sight" (25, 4-5).

As lofty as is this view of God, it is not different from the biblical experience; it has become an objectivized concept arranged to enter into our intellectual and moral standards.

Job's friends vainly strive to express the divine transcendence, but they unconsciously bring everything down to their own level. When Job admits that nothing is holy in God's eyes (9, 20), and maintains his innocence cannot be contested by men, he has to remind them that no man can judge his equal and accuse him of sin, for then he sets himself up as God.

His interlocutors even come to a point where they specify what the Almighty's conduct must be: "This is the wicked man's portion from God, the heritage decreed for him by God" (20, 29).

God's universal knowledge, hidden behind the thick clouds (22, 13), and his absolute omnipotence are thus placed at the service of their human way of judging all things. There is not much difference between the primitive savage placating the forces of nature and civilized man who makes a policeman out of God to protect the good!

❉    ❉    ❉

Job opposes the truth which his own direct experience had taught him of the divinity to these deviations.

It is not Yahweh who must borrow his ideas from his people, but the latter must enter into those of its God. Yahweh is not an abstraction with which the human mind can play, rather the living one who demands all from man and to whom one must give all. Job well understood this truth, for he felt himself carried off by the sovereign will that rendered an account to no one. All-powerful and free, Yahweh pursues a plan known only to himself: "With God are wisdom and might; he has counsel and understanding. If he tears down, none can rebuild; if he shuts a man in, none can open. If he withholds the waters, they dry up; if he sends them out, they overwhelm the land. With him are strength and wisdom; the deceived and the deceiver are his. He leads counselors away stripped, and judges he makes fools. He looses the bonds of kings, and binds a waistcloth on their loins. He leads priests away stripped, and overthrows the mighty. He deprives of speech those who are trusted, and takes away the discernment of elders. He pours contempt on princes, and looses the belt of the strong. He uncovers the deeps out of darkness, and brings deep darkness to light. He makes nations great, and he destroys them; he enlarges nations, and leads them away" (12, 13-23).

Israel seems to be summed up here by the poet. In his mind, as in the memory of the Jews, the Babylonian Exile stands out so vividly that he cannot limit the meaning of the divine interventions to the simple desire of setting up justice among men. Did not Yahweh, since the desert experience, show himself to the Hebrews as an impetuous Master able to turn things at will, tearing away and drawing things irresistibly to himself? "He removes the mountains, and they know it not, when he overturns them in his anger; who shakes the earth out of its place, and its pillars tremble; who commands the sun, and it does not rise; who seals up the stars. . . . Lo, he passes by me, and I see him not; he moves on, but I do not perceive him. Behold, he snatches away; who can hinder him? Who will say to him, 'What doest thou?'" (9, 5-7, 11-12).

Much more than that of his antagonists, the God of Job is the jealous God of the Bible, the indispensable master of Israel's destiny. His strong hand leads the Elect through untrodden and awesome paths, from which it is not good to stray.

The chosen ones advance along these paths with repugnance. The horizon is hidden from them, they cannot see the goal, and they are frightened by the obstacles they meet. Those who do not understand them pursue them with contempt and hatred. Filled with anguish they cry out to Yahweh, and their cry is all the more distressing because they feel it will not be answered. What is there to understand, and what reply is to be expected? There is nothing else to do but follow the road traced out, to follow it with the perfect abandonment of *confidence*.

Elijah stretches out under a tree in the desert, and cries out in his discouragement: "It is enough; now, Oh Lord, take away my life; for I am no better than my fathers" (1 Kgs. 19, 4). "Arise and eat, else the journey will be too great for you" (*Ibid.* 7). He must continue in spite of his fatigue.

Jeremiah felt no less fatigued when he begged God to relinquish his hold: "But thou, O Lord, knowest me; thou seest me, and triest my mind toward thee" (Jer. 12, 3). Yahweh replies: "If you have raced with men on foot, and they have wearied you, how will you compete with horses? And if in a safe land you fall down, how will you do in the jungle of the Jordan?" (Jer. 12, 5). This is the difficulty of the vocation, setting forth its demands, but promising also its rewards: "If you return, if you utter what is precious, and not what is worthless, you shall be in my mouth. . . . And I will make you to all this people a fortified wall of bronze" (Jer. 15, 19-20).

Like others, Job asks for mercy. Answering his long cry of distress, the God of Sinai appears in the tempest. Far from explaining or justifying himself, he orders him to rise and continue the journey. Job, confident of justice, calls upon God; but to his complaints God grants him only one statement: the transcendence of his action. Job loses all self-assurance and bows down before him. He realizes that with God there is no other way of acting but by a complete surrendering to the hand that inflicts pain while it guides and sustains him.

✿    ✿    ✿

What does Yahweh say of himself? We have only to listen to his answer to learn that everything must bend to his will. The whole creation obeys him at a signal. The tempestuous sea is under his control; the dawn takes up its post; light and darkness go to their respective places; hail is kept in reserve for the day of combat; the lightning springs forth from the clouds; and the mass of waters in the skies bursts upon the thirsty soil. The divine will is worked from the heavens upon earthly beings. It furnishes the lion with his prey, procures wide open spaces for the wild ass, gives strength to the horse, and to the eagle it opens up inaccessible heights. In this universal movement man finds himself hemmed in on all sides. Will he alone, then, refuse to be carried by the breath of the Almighty?

This is the question Yahweh asks Job: "Shall a faultfinder contend with the Almighty? He who argues with God, let him answer it" (40, 2). Job can only bow down: "Behold, I am of small account; what shall I answer thee? I lay my hand on my mouth" (40, 4).

The divine action is not limited to this, for Yahweh has not yet said everything until he reminds Job of his *victory over the forces of evil.*

Yahweh can bend the proud and crush the wicked with a look (40, 11-12). Has he not reduced to impotency the sea monsters of the Babylonian legends? Those monsters who had to be crushed to ensure the world's stability, and who were the very embodiment of opposition to God? Behemoth had to hide in the reeds of the marshes (40, 21-22); his mouth spits fire (41, 10-11), and he sows terror in his path, but before Yahweh he cringes in fear. Yahweh alone can speak fearlessly about these monsters and even amuse himself with them: "Leviathan which thou didst form to sport in the sea" (Ps. 104, 25). So complete is Yahweh's victory over these powers of destruction and pride that Job can only humble himself before him: "I know that thou canst do all things, and that no purpose of thine can be thwarted" (42, 2).

In short, Yahweh is the Demiurge. He rules and gives life to the creation which he has drawn out of nothingness. He is the Judge from whom nothing escapes, and who will pass sentence; the Shepherd who leads his flock towards pastures prepared for it, through paths of his own choosing; the Master who disposes of all things and everyone at his pleasure; the living One, finally, who pursues the dialogue with his Elect to which he has invited them.

                        *   *   *

He invites Israel, in the concluding scene of the drama, to cease questioning its destiny and continue the long exodus leading to an unknown world. How can Israel understand what surpasses its understanding? The mystery of its trial remains a mystery, but it now at least understands the vanity of certain interpretations given it.

It knows now that the weight of trial is not necessarily that of malediction; that it is no reprobate, but rather Yahweh's Servant. It is following a hard itinerary which, though frequently obscure, is traced out by Wisdom herself. Although the goal is beyond its reach, it is arranged by a design of love; and this love is shown by the divine manifestations which mark out its fulfillment.

Yahweh has given his answer. Job, like Elijah and Jeremiah, and Israel with him, have only to rise up from their discouragement, to nourish themselves on the word of God, in order to walk with firm steps on to the next phase of their journey.

### F.- THE IMPENETRABLE MYSTERY OF WISDOM

The Book of Proverbs lays stress upon the transcendency of Wisdom. Far from being a human invention, Wisdom was the first to come from the hands of Yahweh. Man's passing teaching cannot mould her; rather, she influences every man that comes within her reach. It is within her maternal womb that the Elect choose life and becomes personally committed. From the world in which the Elect is born, she raises him up to a world of grace.

This idea becomes much clearer in the Book of Job. While Wisdom directs her disciples' steps on this earth, she is drawing them into another world whose borders are unknown to them.

And she herself is this new world which escapes the understanding of men. Just as the sun bathes everything in its light and yet cannot be directly gazed upon, so Wisdom enlightens all without giving up anything of her mystery: "God understands the way of it, and he knows its place" (28, 23).

This is not the way Job's friends understand Wisdom. Their understanding of her is comparable to their understanding of Yahweh's Justice. Just as they freely expressed their interpretations of Yahweh's judgments, so their claims regarding Wisdom are similarly expressed. They admit that she is impenetrable, but they never cease speaking of her as though they fully understood her secrets: "But oh, that God would speak, and open his lips to you, and that he would tell you the secrets of wisdom! For he is manifold in understanding. Know then that God exacts of you less than your guilt deserves" (11, 5-6).

Their white beards attest to a long and true experience. They have gathered together immemorial traditions, and this is their boast: "Are you the first man that was born? Or were you brought forth before the hills? Have you listened to the council of God? And do you limit wisdom to yourself? What do you know that we do not know? What do you understand that is not clear to us? Both the gray-haired and the aged are among us, older than your father" (15, 7-10).

Eliphaz, in his reverence for the antiquity of these venerable traditions, too easily confounds the empiric wisdom with which they are filled with the Wisdom that was created before the world. In this he is mistaken. Without hesitation he parallels the sweetness which comes from God and the suavity of his own remonstrances: "Are the consolations of God too small for you, or the word that deals gently with you?" (15, 11).

His statements are to be accepted as the very words of Yahweh. It does not enter his mind that Yahweh may speak a different language from his. He boldly concludes one of his discourses thus: "Receive instruction from his mouth, and lay up his words in your heart" (22, 22).

This claim is emphatically rejected by Job. Man is not within his rights when he acts in God's place. Man's wisdom is not God's Wisdom. Though it is true that "wisdom is with the aged" (12, 12), yet Job insists that this wisdom is only human and fragile as are all things human. "No doubt you are the people, and wisdom will die with you!" (12, 2).

Let not human wisdom flatter itself with solving questions. Human suffering, for example, inspires this wisdom with definite judgments and suggests an infallible cure. Its knowledge is summed up in the terse saying which it deems unanswerable: sin engenders misfortune; conversion restores interior peace and prosperity.

Job's companions do not fail to apply his principle to him: "Behold, you have instructed many, and you have strengthened weak hands. Your words have upheld him who was stumbling, and you made firm the feeble knees. But now it has come to you, and you are impatient; it touches you, and you are dismayed" (4, 3-5).

Job rejects both the statement and its application. His friends may be irritated with his obstinacy: "Surely vexation kills the fool, and jealousy slays the simple" (5, 2), but he will never submit to their simple wisdom. He feels it is too short-sighted to be capable of solving the problem of suffering.

First, optimism, which comes so easily to those who have everything, is powerless to appease the affliction of those whom life has crushed. How can one complain when he lacks nothing? "Does the wild ass bray when he has grass, or the ox low over his fodder?" (6, 5). On the contrary, how can one be silent when everything has been taken away from him? "Therefore, I will not restrain my mouth; I will speak in the anguish of my spirit; I will complain in the bitterness of my soul" (7, 11).

Advisers are at ease when they are not troubled, but one must experience suffering himself if he is to be able to speak of it wisely. "I also could speak as you do, if you were in my place;

I could join words together against you, and shake my head at you. I could strengthen you with my mouth, and the solace of my lips would assuage your pain. If I speak, my pain is not assuaged, and if I forbear, how much of it leaves me?" (16, 4-6).

In the absence of personal experience, one must observe an evil closely in order to cure it. Shut up within the narrow confines of their own lack of experience and their ways of thinking, these friends of Job are incapable of making any kind of diagnosis since they refuse to consider the facts: "I will teach you concerning the hand of God; what is with the Almighty I will not conceal. Behold, all of you have seen it yourselves; why then have you become altogether vain?" (27, 11-12).

The infortunate one, at grips with the inexplicable, must expect no help from these narrow-minded sages, these *"worthless physicians"* (13, 4), who have only *"maxims of ashes"* to offer (13, 12).

We can easily understand Job's exasperation when answering Bildad: "How you have helped me who have no power! How you have saved the arm that has no strength! How you have counseled him that has no wisdom, and plentifully declared sound knowledge! With whose help have you uttered words, and whose spirit has come forth from you?" (26, 2-4).

Let men's wisdom be silent in the presence of one who is suffering. In spite of their assurances, his friends have expounded only according to their inexperience or their unsound theology. How can they discern Yahweh's plan regarding his Servant?

Job is exhausted trying to fathom this plan, and all the hypotheses he envisions seem filled with vanity. At least he can recognize the weakness of his own wisdom, even before Yahweh reproaches him: "Who is this that darkens counsel by words without knowledge?" (38, 2).

God's Wisdom alone has the right to speak. This Wisdom is beyond the reach of human understanding just as God is. In vain would man, after having probed the secrets of the earth, sound the depths of the starry firmament. Nowhere, in the created order, will he find an explanation of the destiny of those chosen by Yahweh.

This same Wisdom, lost in the impenetrable mystery of the divine plan, promises to nourish them at her table and give them life. But, we repeat, to live with Wisdom is to enter another world: "Whence then comes Wisdom? And where is the place of understanding? It is hid from the eyes of all living, and concealed from the birds of the air. Abaddon and Death say, 'We have heard of it with our ears.' God understands the way of it, and he knows its place" (28, 20-23).

Is this not a rough sketch of the words of Jesus himself: "What is born of the flesh is flesh; what is born of the spirit is spirit" (Jn. 3, 6)?

# THE BOOK OF ECCLESIASTES

3 This book is entitled "Qoheleth" in the Hebrew text, and this can be translated as *"Presidency of the assembly,"* a function devolving upon some doctor of an academy of sages.

Although he introduces himself in the first chapters under the name of Solomon, the author must certainly not be taken literally. Judging by its language, the book of Qoheleth is one of the most recent of the Old Testament books: its redaction is contemporary with the conquests of Alexander (332), if, as is more probable, it is not after these conquests.

The unity of the work was denied for a long time. Recent works, however, have allowed us to revise this judgment and their arguments are solid enough to authorize us to say that Ecclesiastes is the work of one author.

Many passages still remain difficult to understand.

A.- IN PURSUIT OF THE WIND

Ecclesiastes lends itself to many comparisons with both ancient and modern literature. It recalls the ancient pessimistic writings of Egypt. It seems to re-echo the songs of the blind harpist who invites his guests during a banquet to meditate with joy on the pillage of the ancient pyramids and the lot reserved for the dead.

The *panta rei* of Heraclitus is not without analogy in the first chapters of Ecclesiastes. There seems to be a definite influence of Greek philopsophy here, for we are at the dawn of the Hellenistic era and the conquests of Alexander have been instrumental in spreading this philosophy through the Orient.

There are certain modern moralists who may well be compared to Qoheleth. He may be considered as the most modern mind of the Bible. More than one critic has seen in him the bitter disillusionment of the aging civilizations.

These comparisons, however, shed no light on the true physiognomy of the author of Ecclesiastes or on his complex work. Are we dealing with an undeceived sage, a sceptic, or a pleasure-seeker who is attempting to disguise his materialistic views under the cloak of pious words? The complexity of the personage has resulted in a number of exegetes dissecting his work minutely and seeing in it the work of more than one author. Some have counted as many as nine; this number has been reduced to four, and even to two. Exegetes have even come to the point of doubting the advisability of this somewhat arbitrary vivisection, and the more recent commentators try to safeguard both the unity of the work and its author.

It seems to us that the matter can be greatly simplified when we try to place the work in the general line of Israel's thought rather than study the various ideas as though it were a question of analyzing the work of a moralist. True, we shall find in the work certain things known on the shores of the Nile and on the banks of the Aegean Sea. However, the content will remain basically biblical.

We have already remarked that, even when they do not speak of it explicitly, all the sacred writers never lose sight of the Covenant which influences their whole thought. Qoheleth is no exception. We should never separate the problems which occupy them from the fact of the Election. If some find it impossible to see one personage in the diversity of Qoheleth, it is because they have lost sight of this unifying clue which unifies his work: God has placed his hand upon me; where is he leading me?

*  *  *

Qoheleth's apparent pessimism, like the suffering of Job, emphasizes the idea that *life has a direction, an irreversible direction.* Here we have something original, not to be found in the consciousness of humanity. We know that ancient thought was dominated by the myth of constant beginnings. Egypt established its religious concepts on the rotation of night and day, and the agrarian civilizations of eastern Asia on that of the seasons. In Israel, where Yahweh takes a hand in the human destiny of a people or an individual, existence acquires a value without comparison; it becomes the theatre of an experience which is not repeated.

Let it be understood, however, that this life has still only an earthly direction, since it is exclusively in time that the Covenant-drama appears to be enacted. When Yahweh chose his people in the desert, he seemed to have the intention only of giving it a place "in the sun" and of setting its history within the general entanglement of nations. When the privilege of the Election is extended from the community to the individual, these perspectives will not be immediately extended: the Israelite, still unable to see that the hand of God is leading him beyond earthly confines, thinks this divine action is exercised only in the land of the living: "But he who is joined with all the living has hope, for a living dog is better than a dead lion. For the living know that they will die, but the dead know nothing, and they have no more reward; but the memory of them is lost. Their love and their hate and their envy have already perished, and they have no more for ever any share in all that is done under the sun" (9, 4-6).

If then God's Design is realized on earth, in the narrow confines of time, it is from this life alone that one can expect the tangible and durable goods promised by the Covenant. What good is it then to make one's escape beyond this life since in it alone one can expect this good? "As he came from his mother's womb he shall go again, naked as he came, and shall take nothing for his toil, which he may carry away in his hand" (5, 15).

Man's only hope is that God will allow him to realize all the aspirations of his being; if not, then it were better that he had never become involved in the human adventure: "If a man begets a hundred children, and lives many years, so that the days of his years are many, but he does not enjoy life's good things, and also has no burial, I say that an untimely birth is better off than he. For it comes into vanity and goes into darkness, and in darkness its name is covered; moreover it has not seen the sun or known anything; yet it finds rest rather than he. Even though he should live a thousand years twice told, yet enjoy no good — do not all go to the one place?" (6, 3-6).

Because he believes life has a meaning the Israelite loves the *effort* it requires.

However, he expects some *profit* from it even though he loves it. In fact, the Bible has never preached love of work for itself. The divine work was completed on the repose of the Seventh Day. That is why the sage thinks: "Better a handful of quietness than two hands full of toil and a striving after wind" (4, 6).

This profit must be substantial and he must be able to enjoy it personally. How bitter it is for him to realize that the hands that gather it will be those of strangers, perhaps even his enemies! ". . . a man to whom God gives wealth, possessions, and honor, so that he lacks nothing of all that he desires, yet God does not give him power to enjoy them, but a stranger enjoys them; this is vanity; it is a sore affliction" (6, 2). "I hated all my toil in which I had toiled under the sun, seeing that I must leave it to the man who come after me" (2, 18). ". . . because sometimes a man who has toiled with wisdom and knowledge and skill must leave all to be enjoyed by a man who did not toil for it. This also is vanity and a great evil. What has a man from all the toil and strain with which he toils beneath the sun?" (2, 21-22).

Qoheleth gives the lie to this fruitful hope which the Jew has placed on life: nothing here on earth, he says, justifies the feverish activity engaged in by men: "Vanity of vanities, says the Preacher, vanity of vanities! All is vanity. What does a man gain by all the toil at which he toils under the sun?" (1, 2-3).

In fact, what can we expect in a world where everything seems to happen by necessity, where nothing can be changed, and where man is caught up in a web of fate, where, with the regularity of a pendulum, his life swings between antithetical states?

"For everything there is a season, and a time for every matter under heaven: a time to be born, and a time to die; a time to plant, and a time to pluck up what is planted; a time to kill, and a time to heal; a time to break down, and a time to build up; a time to weep, and a time to laugh; a time to mourn, and a time to dance; a time to cast away stones, and a time to gather stones together; a time to embrace, and a time to refrain from embracing; a time to seek, and a time to lose; a time to keep, and a time to cast away; a time to rend, and a time to sew; a time to keep silence, and a time to speak; a time to love, and a time to hate; a time for war, and a time for peace" (3, 1-8).

These reflections may seem meaningless, but when we think of the feverish activity of the Jew, how sadly must they have resounded within the depths of Israel's soul! Why trouble to build today what inevitably will be destroyed tomorrow? The chosen people count on the flowering of a new era in which men on earth will be transfigured, but what an illusion this is! "What has been is what will be, and what has been done is what will be done; and there is nothing new under the sun" (1, 9).

In short, the universe and the constant succession of its changes, comparable to the waves of the ocean, are no justification for man's dream and cannot nourish his hopes or stimulate his ambitions: "A generation goes, and a generation comes, but the earth remains for ever. The sun rises and the sun goes down, and hastens to the place where it rises. The wind blows to the south, and goes round to the north; round and round goes the wind, and on its circuits the wind returns. All streams run to the sea, but the sea is not full; to the place where the streams flow, there they flow again. All things are full of weariness; a man cannot utter it; the eye is not satisfied with seeing, nor the ear filled with hearing" (1, 4-8).

Does this mean that Qoheleth breaks here with the biblical concept of the universe and the irreversible direction of creation in order to comply with the idea of "monotonous" repetition of events as held by the ancient civilizations? We may be very much tempted to believe this, but this is not so. Although the Babylonians and Egyptians believed in this constant repetition of nature, it still did not bother them because they did not find it tedious. On the other hand, Qoheleth is exasperated by this movement leading nowhere because he is conscious of Israel's history of continual progress.

If only this fatal alternation would allow the deserving man some kind of reward! But, here again, all is vanity. Let a man be swift in the race, strong in the fight, clever in business, good virtuous, and even wise, he still will not be free from these setbacks and disappointment. "Again I saw that under the sun the race is not to the swift, nor the battle to the strong, nor bread to the wise, nor riches to the intelligent, nor favor to men of skill; but time and chance happen to them all" (9, 11).

Since this is so, what advantage is there to be wise instead of foolish? "So I turned to consider wisdom and madness and folly; for what can the man do who comes after the king? Only what he has already done. Then I saw that wisdom excels folly as light excels darkness. The wise man has his eyes in his head, but the fool walks in darkness; and yet I perceived that one fate is to all of them. Then I said to myself, 'What befalls the fools will befall me also; why then have I been so very wise?'" (2, 12-15).

Proceeding a little further with this pitiless analysis, Ecclesiastes makes the supposition that, contrary to all probability, man does realize his heart's aspirations and success does crown his efforts. But even all this is still nothing but wind which he holds in his hands. Riches will be only a source of bitterness for him; he will still lose his sleep trying to guard them or else he will be cheated by swindlers: "When goods increase, they increase who eat them; and what gain has their owner but to see them with his eyes?" (5, 11).

What about the much praised splendor of Solomon? Does not the Bible look upon it as the fruit of the wisdom the king had begged from Yahweh? Setting himself in the king's place, Qoheleth makes a swift inventory of the happiness seemingly connected with his reign: "I said to myself, 'Come now, I will make a test of pleasure; enjoy yourself.' But behold, this also was vanity. I said of laughter, 'It is mad,' and of pleasure, 'What use is it?' I searched with my mind how to cheer my body with wine, my mind still guiding me with wisdom, and how to lay hold on folly, till I might see what was good for the sons of men to do under heaven during the few days of their life. I made great works; I built houses and planted vineyards for myself; I made myself gardens and parks, and planted in them all kinds of fruit trees. I made myself pools with which to water the forest of growing trees. I bought male and female slaves, and had slaves who were born in my house; I had also great possessions of herds and flocks, more than any who had been before me in Jerusalem. I also gathered for myself silver and gold and the treasures of kings and provinces; I got singers, both men and women, and many concubines, man's delight. So I became great and surpassed all who were before me in Jerusalem; also my wisdom remained with me. And whatever my eyes desired I did not keep from them; I kept my heart from no pleasure, for my heart found pleasure in all my toil, and this was my reward for all my toil. Then I considered all that my hands had done and the toil I had spent in doing it, and behold, all was vanity and a striving after wind, and there was nothing to be gained under the sun" (2, 1-11).

Qoheleth hits against the wall which imprisons him within a cold and empty world, and there is no place for hope. Such is the lot of humanity; such is Israel's also, obsessed as it is by an empty dream and living in an imaginary future which can bring nothing. Israel is in pursuit of nothing but the wind!

And this is exactly what Qoheleth wants to bring out: Israel's mistake lies in hoping for too much from this life, in giving itself up to dreams that are as inordinate as they are inconstant.

*  *  *

Is this really a pessimistic attitude? No, rather, it is clear-sightedness which reduces to nothing all ambitions and desires that are purely terrestrial. More than one Jewish soul must have shuddered at this revelation of the sage. But this revelation was extremely salutary. Israel's teaching was about to be made to surpass itself in one great stride: it was forced into the necessity of looking upon the existence of another world, a world which would extends its horizons into infinity.

And cannot even modern man, the Christian not excepted, draw profit from the severe examination to which the sage submits the dreams and the desires of the Jew? The chill experienced by the Jew upon reading Qoheleth is still both useful and beneficial for us today!

### B.- VALUE OF THE PRESENT MOMENT

Although Qoheleth has burst Israel's earthly dreams like a balloon, it does not mean that he has lost the meaning of the Covenant. Because he plainly teaches the emptiness of temporal goods and their pursuit, it does not follow that he is preaching some form of listlessness with regard to these things. All is vanity, true, but the Elect is under the hand of God who continues to sustain him.

In Ecclesiastes there is something totally different from a teaching that is either negative or destructive. We have not always been aware of this. It contains a positive teaching which shows clearly the action of God's influence over man.

Among the hasty judgments which the book has produced, there is one which has been stressed as much as it has been minimized; and we should give it our prompt attention: Qoheleth, some have said, would be a free-thinker, a sceptic, or an indifferentist in matters religious. In spite of their pious flavor, what is to be said of his statements concerning the Most High? They appear to be entirely out of place in the book as a whole and to be such as to belie the opinion that has been expressed. This does not seem to hold true, so some are quick to overcome the difficulty by having recourse to the theory that there was more than one author involved.

Qoheleth's piety can be surprising; it is nevertheless sincere. Actually it in no way resembles traditional piety. It manifests a new orientation which will greatly influence Jewish thought: it reveals and brings to the fore the religious value of the *present moment*.

* * *

One generally thinks the religion of Ecclesiastes is characterized by the desire to avoid all excess: here, as elsewhere, its wisdom would guard against all useless trouble. But to think this way would be to understand poorly its teaching and well as to reduce its religion to lukewarmness.

The sage, it is true, recommends that we do not multiply offerings and lose ourselves in long prayers in Yahweh's presence. He tells us not to be too anxious in making vows: "Guard your steps when you go to the house of God; to draw near to listen is better than to offer the sacrifice of fools; for they do not know that they are doing evil. Be not rash with your mouth, nor let your heart be hasty to utter a word before God, for God is in

heaven, and you upon earth; therefore let your words be few"
(5, 1-2).

Counsel is suggested by nothing else but the *fear of Yahweh*:
". . . why should God be angry at your voice, and destroy the
work of your hands? For when dreams increase, empty words
grow many: but do you fear God!" (5, 5-6).

Sacrifices, prayers, and vows can sometimes be the expression
of man's dissatisfaction and his desire to escape. To desert the
present is tantamount to flight from God, for God's empire is
revealed in the little, humble moment that is passing by. Man
should not be preoccupied by what has happened or will happen,
but he should accept what is actually happening now.

It is vanity to compare the present with what has ceased to
be: "In the day of prosperity be joyful, and in the day of adversity consider; God has made the one as well as the other, so
that man may not find out anything that will be after him"
(7, 14). "Say not, 'Why were the former days better than these?'
For it is not from wisdom that you ask this" (7, 10).

Again, it is vanity to distract oneself from the present moment
that belongs to us in order to wander into the uncertain mists
of the future which are deceiving. We should keep in mind how
all human enterprises end: ". . . and the patient in spirit is better
than the proud in spirit" (7, 8). "It is better to go to the house
of mourning than to go to the house of feasting; for this is the
end of all men, and the living will lay it to heart" (7, 2).

Is man certain his destiny will advance beyond that of the
beast? "I said in my heart with regard to the sons of men that
God is testing them to show them that they are but beasts. For
the fate of the sons of men and the fate of beasts is the same; as
one dies, so dies the other. They all have the same breath, and
man has no advantage over beasts; for all is vanity. All go to one
place; all are from the dust, and all turn to dust again. Who
knows whether the spirit of man goes upward and the spirit of
the beast goes down to the earth?" (3, 18-21).

Without being obsessed by the future and without regret for

the past, let the wise man profit from life such as it is given to him at present: "Go, eat your bread with enjoyment, and drink your wine with a merry heart; for God has already approved what you do. Let your garments be always white; let not oil be lacking on your head. Enjoy life with the wife whom you love, all the days of your vain life which has been given you under the sun, because that is your portion in life and in your toil at which you toil under the sun. Whatever your hand finds to do, do it with your might; for there is no work or thought or knowledge or wisdom in Sheol, to which you are going" (9, 7-10).

Another error would be deducing from such a text that Qoheleth was either a hedonist or an Epicurean. His thought lends itself to no philosophic system. Far from being an apology for pure enjoyment, his teaching contains the *accepting of the present life,* not only with its satisfactions, but also with its trials and pains.

Although Qoheleth dissuades man from striving indiscriminately after unattainable goals, yet he in no way encourages him to be idle: "The fool folds his hands, and eats his own flesh" (4, 5).

In the biblical *"carpe diem"* there is no exclusion from toil. Man is to seek his happiness where he finds it, even in the weariness of work. "There is nothing better for a man than that he should eat and drink and find enjoyment in his toil" (2, 24; cf. 3, 13; 5, 17; 8, 15).

It is even in this labor that Solomon consoled himself in all his disillusionments: ". . . my heart found pleasure in all my toil, and this was my reward for all my toil" (2, 10).

The dynamism of the Israelite soul is then not so radically attained as it appears; it is destined to play itself out within the restricted limits of the present moment. Far from discouraging activity, the uncertainty of the morrow suggests that one should not foolishly depend upon it. One should perform his duty without any illusion and without any fanciful planning: "As you do not know how the spirit comes to the bones in the womb of a woman with child, so you do not know the work of God who makes everything. In the morning sow your seed, and in the evening withhold your hand; for you do not know which will prosper, this or that, or whether both alike will be good" (11, 5-6).

As we see, this is totally relative hedonism. But we still must add that the sage's reflections are inspired by a deep feeling of the *"gift of God."* This expression is too frequently repeated for one to suppose that it belongs to considerations entirely devoid of all religious significance. Man is no longer able to see the blessings God bestows upon him because of his feverish pursuit of unstable dreams. " Remember also your Creator in the days of your youth, before the evil days come, and the years draw nigh, when you will say, 'I have no pleasure in them' " (12, 1).

Israel until now has always shown itself attentive in praising God for all its past blessings. Its confidence in the future and its gratitude are founded upon the remembrance of Yahweh's great deed. Before Ecclesiastes there seem to be almost absent from the sacred text both the consciousness of the actuality of the divine gift and the idea of showing a joyful gratitude for it.

We can, then, on this point, salute in Qoheleth an innovator. The care with which he emphasizes the value of the present moment prepares (remotely, for he is neither explicit nor is he fully aware of its value) for the Christian notion of the *actuality of salvation.* Acknowledgment of the divine gift extended to the most humble realities of existence, their joyous acceptance, and constant thankfulness for them will not be the characteristics simply of a particular type of spirituality, like that of St. Francis of Assisi, but of the entire christian spirit, which is built only on the gradual discovery of a twofold void: that of a past that no longer belongs to man and a future that still belongs to God. This spirit is built also upon that long work of detachment which allows one to discern in the precious present moment the unique opportunity of making one's encounter with God.

Let us point out also how opportune is this evaluation of the present moment since the advent of Marxism. The christian idea of history is strongly opposed to the Hegelian notion of development: on the route of the future, the present is not a simple relay station; each generation is not destined, after having come to maturity, to serve as fertilizer for future generations, but rather each possesses in itself an absolute value. The future, furthermore, to use another figure of speech, will add new links to the chain of generations only if the preceding links are solidly forged; otherwise, how can there be a solid chain?

The gift of God is constantly renewed in each successive moment, the coherence of which goes to make up the unity of human life. And their compactness is such that it is in this present moment that the drama of the soul is played out and that its eternal destiny is being prepared. "If you but knew the gift of God" (John 4, 10).

C.- WISDOM IS BEYOND THE REACH OF MAN

To know how to recognize in the present moment the divine gift evidently does not solve the problem of evil. Qoheleth was aware of this.

Israel was awaiting the establishment of a kingdom of justice and peace from the hand that was guiding it. Its first sages had promised it the enjoyment of the fruit of its labor and the reward of its trials in the immediate future. Job had, however, observed that Wisdom does not obey the laws of our mind, but remains hidden in mystery. Qoheleth goes even further: not only is she a stranger to this world, but she is beyond our reach.

There is, consequently, no remedy for evil, whether it springs from the awkwardness of man or from the disposition of God: "What is crooked cannot be made straight..." (1, 15). "Consider the work of God; who can make straight what he has made crooked?" (7, 13).

Although evil is inevitable, one can conceive of living as if it did not exist. Philosophical systems had made the attempt: the Stoic denies its existence; the Epicure seeks distraction from it;

and the Buddhist flees from it. Such is not Qoheleth's attitude. He does not try to put to sleep the consciousness of evil; his realism persists in looking upon the world with a clear and a courageous glance: "Again I saw all the oppressions that are practiced under the sun. And behold, the tears of the oppressed, and they had no one to comfort them! On the side of their oppressors there was power, and there was no one to comfort them. And I thought the dead who are already dead more fortunate than the living who are still alive; but better than both is he who has not yet been, and has not seen the evil deeds that are done under the sun" (4, 1-3).

The sight is not comforting; but how can one accept it as it is? We cannot deny reality. We must not even be surprised at it: "If you see in a province the poor oppressed and justice and right violently taken away, do not be amazed at the matter . . ." (5, 8).

Everything on earth is subject to *man's whims,* and no authority, to which we may have recourse, has a way of remedying the injustice.

Should we, as did Plato, desire the sages govern the world? Qoheleth does not even think this, as it seems too utopian; men do not listen to Wisdom: "But I say that wisdom is better than might, though the poor man's wisdom is despised and his words are not heeded" (9, 16).

It is, however, prudent to yield when the one speaking is armed with strength; and it is good, if he exercises this strength legitimately: "Keep the king's command, and because of your sacred oath be not dismayed; go from his presence, do not delay when the matter is unpleasant, for he does whatever he pleases" (8, 2-3).

Whatever spectacle the world presents to him, the sage will not sacrifice his security by trusting anyone, even by formulating a judgment within his mind: "Even in your thought, do not curse the king, nor in your bedchamber curse the rich; for a bird of the air will carry your voice, or some winged creature tell the matter" (10, 20).

We see that the sage has hardly any opportunity of playing a role in the State and when he can raise his voice, his beneficent action would be quickly contradicted: "Wisdom is better than weapons of war, but one sinner destroys much good. Dead flies make the perfumers ointment give off an evil odor; so a little folly outweights wisdom and honor" (9, 18; 10, 1).

Thus the world is irremediably given over to force and whim and there is no hope of ever seeing order and harmony prevail, where anarchy alone can reign. Qoheleth's considerations in this matter are an echo of the bitter reflections of the ancient Egyptian sages: "There is an evil which I have seen under the sun, as it were an error proceeding from the ruler: folly is set in many high places, and the rich sit in a low place. I have seen slaves on horses, and princes walking on foot like slaves" (10, 5-7).

If, at least, in this confusion of the social order justice made an exception! But man, even in this divine function, is only servility with regard to his passions and to power: "Moreover I saw under the sun that in the place of justice, even there was wickedness, and in the place of righteousness, even there was wickedness" (3, 16).

From the absence of justice there inevitably flows the most scandalous reversal of values, for merit is not recognized, virtue goes unrewarded, and crime is not punished: "Then I saw the wicked buried; they used to go in and out of the holy place, and were praised in the city where they had done such things.... Because sentence against an evil deed is not executed speedily, the heart of the sons of man is fully set to do evil.... There is a vanity which takes place on earth, that there are righteous men to whom it happens according to the deeds of the wicked, and there are wicked men to whom it happens according to the deeds of the righteous" (8, 10, 11, 14).

Each one is allowed to act according to his fancy. The human condition, abandoned to man's whim, carries the indelible mark of this vice: "... man lords it over man to his hurt" (8, 9).

What about God? Will he not intervene in this disorder? Apparently not: "Everything before them is vanity, since one fate comes to all, to the righteous and the wicked, to the good and the evil, to the clean and the unclean, to him who sacrifices and him who does not sacrifice. As is the good man, so is the sinner; and he who swears is as he who shuns an oath" (9, 2).

In spite of all this, Qoheleth strongly affirms his *faith in divine providence* with regard to the Elect, even though he seems to be enmeshed in the anarchy of this world: "But all this I laid to heart, examining it all, how the righteous and the wise and their deeds are in the hand of God ..." (9, 1).

The contradiction is only apparent. It flows from the truth that God's mind is impenetrable: "I have seen the business that God has given to the sons of men to be busy with. He has made everything beautiful in its time; also he has put eternity into man's mind, yet so that he cannot find out what God has done from the beginning to the end" (3, 10-11).

Man has light enough to be assured that God rules the world, but not enough to understand how: "I know that whatever God does endures for ever; nothing can be added to it, nor anything taken from it; God has made it so, in order that men should fear before him" (3, 14).

It is folly to aspire to know this: "When I applied my mind to know wisdom, and to see the business that is done on earth, how neither day nor night one's eyes see sleep; then I saw all the work of God, that man cannot find out the work that is done under the sun. However much man may toil in seeking, he will not find it out; even though a wise man claims to know, he cannot find it out" (8, 16-17).

Man's destiny is inexplicable. Wisdom surpasses all objects. It is impossible on earth and even useless to seek Wisdom out: "All this I have tested by Wisdom; I said, 'I will be wise'; but it was far from me. That which is, is far off, and deep, very deep; who can find it out?" (7, 23-24).

Man is enclosed in a world where good and evil co-exist and seem to counter-balance each other: "Surely there is not a righteous person on earth who does good and never sins" (7, 20).

How, then, find the ideal Woman here below, the living incarnation of perfection and Wisdom? "One man among a thousand I found, but a woman among all these I have not found" (7, 28). A disappointing conclusion which can seem hopeless. It stands to reason that this work stands in need of an additional revelation; but this very brief work of Ecclesiastes will nonetheless have played a very important role in sapiential literature.

Qoheleth puts an abrupt stop to that foolish thrust which carries the chosen people towards that chimeric conquest of a purely temporal future. He wishes to retain only the inestimable gift of the present moment of the divine activity: everything else appears to escape man and lose itself in the mystery of God.

We find in this book a contradictory avowal of discouragement and constancy, bitterness and sereneness, pessimism and faith. All of which would allow one to believe in a withdrawal of Wisdom. It was necessary that things be such, for Qoheleth felt himself disoriented, and he prepares for the transformation which will support the dream of Israel at the beginning of the second century.

After the peaceful lights of Proverbs and the blinding lights of Job, it appears as though we are about to descend into darkness. At the end of the descent there is a door opening out to flood Jewish thought in waves of virgin light and to uncover those limitless perspectives of the apocalyptic literature.

# THE BOOK OF ECCLESIASTICUS OR
# THE WISDOM OF JESUS THE SON OF SIRACH

**4** The author of Ecclesiasticus is currently known as Sirach or Ben Sira in Hebrew. He was a scribe who was undoubtedly as proud of his profession as he was of the traditions of his own people. He was active at Jerusalem around the beginning of the second century, or to be more exact, between 190 and 170 B.C.

His work, written in Hebrew, was not known directly in the christian tradition. Christians read it in the Greek translation made by the author's grandson. The original text disappeared in the course of the Middle Ages. Someone discovered a manuscript by chance in 1896, which restores two-thirds of the original text. It was buried in the genizah of one of the synagogues in Cairo, the genizah being a storeroom where the Jews kept worn manuscripts of the holy books. Its value, however, is open to dispute.

At any rate, only the Greek text has been and remains canonical and has been received as such by the Church.

A.- ISRAEL BECOMES CONSCIOUS OF ITSELF

Ben Sirach's work, the Book of the Assembly or the "Book of the Church" par excellence, seems so close to us that we cannot say it shocks us; it hardly excites our curiosity.

Can the modern reader, however, be indifferent to the author's bonhomie? There is nothing in Sirach that flatters our imagination and our desire for mystery; yet we find ourselves quickly sympathizing with him, even though we may think the well-balanced, wise, and bourgeois character of the ideal he presents is somewhat amusing. His approach to life is contagious. Although he does not incite us to heroism, his program effectively cuts down the fever of excessive emotionalism.

> "Do you have cattle? Look after them; if they are profitable to you, keep them. Do you have children? Discipline them, and make them obedient from their youth. Do you have daughters? Be concerned for their chastity, and do not show yourself too indulgent with them. Give a daughter in marriage; you will have finished a great task. But give her to a man of understanding. If you have a wife that pleases you, do not cast her out; but do not trust yourself to one whom you detest. With all your heart honor your father, and do not forget the birth pangs of your mother. Remember that through your parents you were born; and what can you give back to them that equals their gift to you? With all your soul fear the Lord, and honor his priests. With all your might love your Maker, and do not forsake his ministers. Fear the Lord and honor the priest, and give him his portion, as is commanded you; the first fruits, and guilt offering, and the gift of the shoulders, the sacrifice of sanctification, and the first fruits of the holy things" (7, 22-32).

This is the dream of the good, wise, and conscientious Jew who knows how to establish order in his life.

✽   ✽   ✽

However, the interest created by the man and his work is not limited to this; their role has greatly influenced the development of the drama in which Judaism's existence is going to be played out. This bourgeois spirit, reflected in Ben Sirach and his work, must be taken as the necessary reaction of a personality threatened by the invasion of one of the most brilliant civilizations.

Until the present, Israel's Wisdom has never had to set herself in opposition or even compare herself with the wisdom of other nations. She was perfectly original; and there are some, as we said, who wrongly judged her as being fundamentally and initially universal in her appeal. Those who believe she offered her lessons to all men in general are deluded, for Wisdom speaks solely to Israel. Though she seems to lay down no mark of distinction between the Jewish milieu and that of the rest of the world, it is because she herself sees no problem. Neither Proverbs, Job, nor Qoheleth claims to be doing anything else but encouraging the Jew to adhere personally to the Covenant, whose demands they both formulate and help him realize the consequences of non-conformity.

But now a new event, *the intrusion of Hellenism,* forces Judaism to clarify its position. It is no longer between wisdom and folly, i.e., between accepting or refusing the Covenant, that the Israelite will have to choose, but between fidelity to the traditions of his ancestors and the acceptance of the new gods, as dangerous as the old ones, for they would make Israel forgetful of its vocation. The influence of Greek culture, philosophy, and civilization was such that it attracted the whole Orient and even Israel had a fascination for it.

*     *     *

To triumph over this, Jewish thought will have to declare itself clearly; and it will not do this without making clear distinctions and opposing something very definite. The traveler, who has crossed over the borders of his own country, has often discovered at a distance the true nature of his own fatherland, thanks to the endless comparisons with the new way of life in a foreign environment in which he now lives.

It is exactly this that has struck Ben Sirach: "I have seen many things in my travels, and I understand more than I can express" (34, 11).

He testifies to how enriching one's sojourn among strangers can be for one *"who applies himself to meditation on the Law of the Most High"*: ". . . he will travel through the lands of foreign nations, for he tests the good and the evil among them" (39, 4).

He acquires there a deep realization of his own personality, a more ardent love of his own country, a growing attachment to his national traditions, and a certain nostalgia for establishing himself once again on his native soil. He runs a certain risk, however: is not a prolonged absence from his country going to engender foregetfulness? Then the stranger would be nothing but one uprooted. Now, in the eyes of the Bible, the wanderer is accursed: "So who will trust a man that has no home, and lodges wherever night finds him?" (39, 27).

This is not, however, the case of our Sage. At a time in its history when Israel prepares to fight in order to remain Israel, we see in Ben Sirach a man who, after having carefully observed the world, congratulates himself on being a Jew and aspires to nothing more than deepening his affiliation with Israel.

If only we attempt to understand him better, we get a better understanding of his role in the approaching struggle.

As an authentic son of Israel, all the virtues of his race are found in him: courage, tenacity, self-control, liberality, uprightness and fidelity, the entire ideal of the Sage, such as it was conceived in the Book of Proverbs.

Ben Sirach has a hatred for falsehood: "A lie is an ugly blot on a man; it is continually on the lips of the ignorant. A thief is preferable to an habitual liar, but the lot of both is ruin. The disposition of a liar brings disgrace . . ." (20, 24-26).

His *uprightness* is evident in clear answers and frank attitudes: "Be steadfast in your understanding, and let your speech be consistent" (5, 10).

His sense of *fidelity* inspires in him an unfailing attachment to the divine Law and a scrupulous respect for the obligations of marriage: "Whoever keeps the law controls his thoughts..." (21, 11). "A man of understanding will trust in the law" (33, 3). "Agreeable in the sight of the Lord and of men is a wife and a husband who live in harmony" (25, 1).

On this last point, the author, as a good moralist, does not fail to add invaluable insights on the *prudence* from which a man must never depart with regard to women (9, 1-9).

Like his predecessors, he recommends *self-mastery* to his disciples: "Guard yourself in every act, for this is the keeping of the commandments" (32, 30). "Do not follow your base desires, but restrain your appetites" (18, 30).

He evidently advises *sobriety* in eating and drinking: "How ample a little is for a well-disciplined man..." (31, 19). "Do not be valiant over wine, for wine has destroyed many" (31, 25).

*Good manners* are to be observed in society: "Eat like a human being what is set before you..." (31, 16).

Like his predecessors, he is careful about too much talking: one is always better off not to become involved with the quarrels of others, with betraying a confidence, and *in knowing how to keep silent*: "Refrain from strife, and you will lessen sins" (28, 8). "Have you heard a word, let it die with you" (19, 10). "A wise man will be silent until the right moment" (20, 7).

For he should never speak except for a good reason: "Be quick to hear and be deliberate in answering" (5, 11). "Do not answer before you have heard" (11, 8).

Even before God, one should not talk in vain discourse: "Do not repeat yourself in your prayer" (7, 14).

\* \* \*

All these traditional qualities preached by Wisdom are to be found in Ben Sirach, but enriched with Israel's steady progress: sentiments are refined and moral demands deepened.

Its psychology is deeper and slightly advanced from former writings. No writer before him had analyzed the secrets of the heart as deeply, e.g., envy and avarice (14, 3-10), revenge (10, 6; 27, 30-28, 7), pride (10, 7-18; 3, 26-29; 7, 4-5), *human respect* (4, 26-27; 20, 22).

The delicacy of the moralist is shown by the special attention he gives to the most exquisite of human feelings: friendship (6, 5-17; 9, 10; 12, 8-18; 13, 1-23; 22, 19-26; 37, 1-6). This delicacy suggested to him certain insights that always hold true on the acquisition of friends: "When you gain a friend, gain him through testing, and do not trust him hastily" (6, 7).

It holds true, also, in the necessary discretion in keeping these friends: "Whoever betrays secrets destroys confidence, and he will never find a congenial friend and keep faith with him; but if you betray his secrets, do not run after him. For as a man destroys his enemy so you have destroyed the friendship of your neighbor" (27, 16-18). "For a wound may be bandaged, and there is reconciliation after abuse, but whoever has betrayed secrets is without hope" (27, 21).

What a boon, then, is friendship! "A faithful friend is a sturdy shelter; he that has found one has found a treasure" (6, 14). "A faithful friend is an elixir of life" (6, 16).

It is true that friendship is merited: "Whoever fears the Lord directs his friendship aright, for as he is, so is his neighbor also" (6, 17).

He is not less exquisite in defining *modesty* as the exact consciousness of one's own worth, and which keeps one away from extreme humility and proud presumption: "Who will honor the man that dishonors his own life?" (10, 29). "Do not seek from the Lord the highest office, nor the seat of honor from the king. Do not assert your righteousness before the Lord, nor display your wisdom before the king. Do not seek to become a judge, lest you be unable to remove iniquity" (7, 4-6). "My son, glorify yourself with humility, and ascribe to yourself honor according to your worth" (10, 28).

If we keep in mind that the ancient Sages, Egyptian or otherwise, were not overly attracted to the virtue of humility, we shall appreciate this man's discernment, for he seems to speak from actual experience.

This psychology supposes a very personal sensibility. Ben Sirach, in fact, requires an atmosphere of benevolence and *sympathy*: "Make yourself beloved in the congregation . . ."(4, 7).

He has a very personal way of recalling the respect due to the humble, the poor, and the tried: "Incline your ear to the poor, and answer him peaceably and gently. Be like a father to the orphans, and as good as a husband to the widows" (4, 8, 10). "Do not fail those who weep, but mourn with those who mourn. Do not shrink from visiting a sick man . . ." (7, 34-35).

He even understood that to receive pardon from God, man must *pardon* others. "Forgive your neighbor for the wrong he has done, and then your sins will be pardoned when you pray. Does a man harbor anger against another, and yet seek for healing from the Lord? Does he have no mercy towards a man like himself, and yet pray for his own sins? If he himself, being flesh, maintains wrath, who will make expiation for his sins?" (28, 2-5).

Does not the ancient morality of the Sages seem to have reached the vigil of the new era when the law of the Gospel will be promulgated? However, the time of self-donation and the folly of the Cross has not yet arrived; the time when the disciple will be mature enough to understand the meaning of those strange words: *"He who loses his soul will save it. . . ."* In fact, two long centuries still separate Israel from the conclusion of the New Covenant.

For the time being, the Israelite has only to take stock of his spiritual heritage and its richness to be saved. No matter how high his ideals, it is good balance he seeks, rather than heroism. Facing the influences that threaten him today, he has enough to do in taking up a defensive position.

                        ✿   ✿   ✿

We cannot imagine, under these circumstances, a personage more providential than Ben Sirach. With his good qualities and his narrowness, he is really the man of the hour.

In him the vital impulse is wisely controlled by a certain middle-class prudence; the instinct of self-preservation keeps him back from every useless risk.

It is not that he is incapable of *liberality*. Although he feels that he himself should be the first to profit from anything: "My son, treat yourself according to your means. . . . Do not deprive yourself of a happy day; let not your share of the desired good pass by you" (14, 11, 14), yet he advises that one avoid any selfishness and meanness when there is question of dealing with a guest or making an offering for the Temple or leaving something to a friend: "Men will praise the man who is liberal with food . . ." (31, 23). "With every gift show a cheerful face, and dedicate your tithe with gladness" (35, 9). "Do good to your friend before you die, and reach out and give him as much as you can" (14, 13).

But this liberality is not to be exercised except for a good reason: "If you do a kindness, know to whom you do it, and you will be thanked for your good deeds" (12, 1).

It will never compromise, however, one's personal security: "Assist your neighbor according to your ability, but take heed to yourself lest you fall" (29, 20).

For nothing must be more dear to the Sage than his *own*

*home*. No matter how lowly it may be, it is still there that he will find happiness most surely. Elsewhere, hospitality is a rather uncertain affair: "Better is the life of a poor man under the shelter of his roof than sumptuous food in another man's house" (29, 22; cf. 40, 28). "These things are hard to bear for a man who has feeling: scolding about lodging, and the reproach of the money lender" (29, 28; cf. 40, 29).

Many responsibilities await him at home. When recounting these, Ben Sirach departs from that usual good nature of his. The Sage must know how to govern his slaves with a firm and humane hand: "Set your slave to work and you will rest; leave his hands idle, and he will seek liberty" (33, 25). "If you have a servant, treat him as a brother, for as your own soul you will need him" (33, 32).

Again, one must bring up one's sons and daughters strictly: "He who loves his son will whip him often, in order that he may rejoice at the way he turns out" (30, 1). "Keep a strict watch over a headstrong daughter lest she make you a laughingstock to your enemies" (42, 11).

If his wife is wise and good, he should give her his confidence and consideration: "Do not be jealous of the wife of your bosom, and do not teach her an evil lesson to your own hurt" (9, 1).

But if she is wicked, indocile, or talkative, he will repudiate her: "If she does not go as you direct, separate her from yourself" (25, 26).

He should not live, in any way, at her expense, so as not to be led by her: "There is wrath and imprudence and great disgrace when a wife supports her husband" (25, 22). "Do not give yourself to a woman so that she gains mastery over your strength" (9, 2).

He should never surrender to anyone the authority he himself enjoys: "While you are still alive and have breath in you, do not let anyone take your place" (33, 20).

He must preserve the integrity of his patrimony: ". . . and not give his property to another, lest you change your mind and must ask for it" (33, 20).

He should choose his intimate friends: "Do not bring every man into your home, for many are the wiles of the crafty" (11, 29).

He is to be, in a word, in all his rights and duties, complete master of his own home: "At the time you end the days of your life, in the hour of death, distribute your inheritance" (33, 23).

On the other hand, he is not to meddle in things not pertaining to himself: "Do not argue about a matter that does not concern you, nor sit with sinners when they judge a case" (11, 9).

When directly provoked, he will undoubtedly not allow himself or his family to be insulted, but it is better to avoid the company of the uncouth person: "Do not jest with an ill-bred person, lest your ancestors be disgraced" (8, 4).

To avoid all trouble, he should never come in conflict with one more rich and powerful than he is: "Do not go to law against a judge, for the decision will favor him because of his standing" (8, 14). "Do not lift a weight beyond your strength, nor associate with a man mightier and richer than you. How can the clay pot associate with the iron kettle? The pot will strike against it, and will itself be broken" (13, 2).

Has not one everything to lose when frequenting the company of the proud man (13, 1), the fool (8, 17), the angry man (8, 16), and the adventurer (8, 15)? "Whoever touches pitch will be defiled" (13, 1).

Is this not the *manual of the perfect middle-class person?* Ben Sirach's attachment to his own hearth, his opposition to anything that would trouble it in the least, the wise and jealous care of his authority, his generosity that never goes out of bounds, his urbanity which never compromises him, finally, that retirement within his own little world which is certainly not a sign of indifference to whatever is strange to him, but the desire of protecting what is his own. All this sums up very well what we praise in the middle-class person, but also what we find somewhat blameworthy. And it was exactly this that, at the beginning of the second century before Christ, the author of Ecclesiasticus was teaching to his co-religionists.

*     *     *

But he must be on his guard! Let the Israelite know that he is always threatened: "Know that you are walking in the midst of snares, and that you are going about on the city battlements" (9, 13). Undoubtedly, Ben Sirach would be thinking of Israel's danger. Perhaps, measuring the risks run by too many people to whom the most brilliant culture was dazzling, he was presenting in an indistinct manner the misfortunes which the priests at the court of Antiochus would soon engender. But, whether he had this foreknowledge or not, when defending the hearth, it is rather Israel's stability, independence, and integrity that he is effectively protecting. The lesson concerning the careful bourgeois holds good for the nation: "All living beings associate by species, and man clings to one like himself" (13, 16).

This clear and touchy *circumspection*, so careful in judging the value of everything, in screening out all deleterious influences, so prompt in taking refuge in one's natural milieu and in avoiding all discomfort and dangers, is not more inspired by pusillanimity than by a certain inferiority complex: the prudence, even the distrust of which it gives testimony, will turn out to be only too justified.

Israel, like Ben Sirach, is not unaware of its worth. Compared today to the great and victorious Macedonian, as yesterday to the great empires that encircled it, Israel realizes it is a small people, but it also recalls that it is the People of God: "The bee is small among flying creatures, but her product is the best of sweet things" (11, 3).

If anyone has to blush, it is over his sins: "Be ashamed of immorality, before your father or mother; and of a lie, before a prince or a ruler; and of a transgression, before a judge or a magistrate; and of iniquity, before a congregation or a people" (41, 17-18). However, one must never be ashamed of the sacred deposit entrusted to one: "Of the following things do not be ashamed . . . of the law of the Most High and his covenant, and of rendering judgment to acquit the ungodly" (42, 2).

This is a grave statement and a quarter of a century later the Jew will be invited to uphold it with his life.

Israel will have to answer its adversaries and will know what to say, but it would be absurd to advance the time: "There is one who keeps silent because he has no answer, while another keeps silent because he knows when to speak" (20, 6).

Circumspection, in this case, is not cowardly action but rather a powerful weapon which Israel is forging under the advice of the Sage.

We understand the place, therefore, reserved for the Book of Ecclesiasticus in the history of the Jewish religion; no one is better qualified than Ben Sirach to prepare Israel to face up to the difficult struggle. He teaches it that it will be victorious on two conditions: *each* will have to fight as though he alone were withstanding the enemy's attack; all will not withstand the enemy unless they strengthen their *solidarity*.

The Jew will be exposed to danger all alone, for it is within each one's heart that the contest will be played out. Each Jew will have to make his own decisions without the directives of a civil or religious authority which, assuming all responsibility, will leave him with only the duty to obey.

Undoubtedly, there will be no lack of advisers. However, though it is good to seek the advice of the prudent man, one must know how to choose the proper one; it is up to each not to make a mistake: "Be wary of the counselor. . . . But stay constantly with a godly man whom you know to be a keeper of the commandments" (37, 8, 12).

Ben Sirach offered Israel many precious words of advice on

the domestic level, and it has not difficult to make the transition to the spiritual level.

In the final analysis, the Jew will have to take counsel from himself and from God speaking in the depths of his heart: "And establish the counsel of your own heart, for no one is more faithful to you than it is. For a man's soul sometimes keeps him better informed than seven watchmen sitting high on a watchtower. And besides all this pray to the Most High that he may direct your way in truth" (37, 13-15).

In the approaching battle each one will be Israel's champion, as though there were only himself holding its positions and defending its honor, independence, and the integrity of its patrimony.

As effective as this personal commitment may be, the Jew still remains a member of a community. This community is with him, not only to unite him to a necessary social order, but also to pursue a most magnificent and difficult goal.

From this comes the need of joining hands in Israel. Sects are about to make their appearance in which hearts, minds, and wills will be united around one identical ideal. While waiting, the entire people is invited to maintain itself closely grouped around its spiritual riches, as the Hebrews formerly were gathered round the Ark: "As much as you can, aim to know your neighbors, and consult with the wise. Let your conversation be with men of understanding, and let all your questions be about the Law of the Most High. Let righteous men be your dinner companions, and let your glorifying be in the fear of the Lord" (9, 14-16).

Hence arises that important role assigned to friendship by Ben Sirach; it is the strongest bond uniting men together: "Do not exchange a friend for money, or a real brother for the gold of Ophir" (7, 18).

The day will come when the Church of Christ will sustain her martyrs with the warmth of fraternal love. In a future much closer, the Jews, at grips with a civilization both dangerous and admirable, will find strength and consolation in the consciousness of their solidarity and in the support of friendship.

B.- THE PRIVILEGE OF WISDOM AND THE SEARCH FOR HUMAN UNITY

Thus, at a time when Greek civilization and culture are about to submerge the Near East, the Book of Ben Sirach prepares Israel which is sufficiently conscious of its worth so that it will not allow itself to be swallowed up.

This was not the first time that the Chosen People, strong in the privilege of their election, had withstood the unifying force of history. They owed their success in this to their prophets and their allies of the Temple and royal house. Already Israel had reached to the gods of Canaan; already David's small kingdom in the Fertile Crescent had been one of the last States to succumb to the attacks of the invaders from Assyria and Babylon. Even then, in spite of the frightful crisis of the seventh century, branded by Zephaniah and Jeremiah, and even into the Exile itself, the best part of Israel was fiercely obstinate in safeguarding its personality and in believing in the independence of its absolute destiny.

But now, since the Macedonian invasion Jewish exclusiveness will have to face up to an entirely new type of imperialism and a new type of danger. While other conquerors were content with imposing their military, social, and political domination upon the vanquished, along with the dangerous presence of their pantheon, Alexander, who had not forgotten the teachings of Aristotle, intends to bend the minds of the Barbarians and render them pliant to a wisdom with universal pretentions.

Hence it was inevitable that the Jews themselves would one day be called upon to welcome the civilization of the conqueror and to commune, with the rest of the world in the ideal he made of beauty, truth, and humanism.

Israel was not immediately aware of its danger. In the dividing of the immense empire which followed the death of the

Conqueror, Palestine fell to the lot of the Egyptian Ptolemies. These latter were not interested in the dream of Hellenization entertained by Alexander. It was enough for the Greeks to live peacefully with the natives without intermingling with them. The Jews remained among themselves and were not disturbed by the presence of these foreigners.

The situation soon underwent a total change. At the time when Ben Sirach was working on his book, Judea was in the process of changing its rulers. The Seleucids of Antioch were about to succeed the Ptolemies, and these Seleucids did not have the experience of reigning over a homogeneous territory. It appeared to Antiochus III that the only way to bring about unity was to impose Hellenization upon all. He set to work and was very successful, except in the case of the Jews who opposed his efforts with great energy. The more obstinate the Seleucids became, the more the Jews were hardened in their determination to preserve spiritual autonomy. They were resolved never to be dispossessed of the Wisdom which they regarded as the best part of their patrimony.

* * *

Sirach must be looked upon as the first builder of this resistance which, in spite of the disproportion of the contending forces, would end in victory for the Jews.

Their intransigence can be explained only by their enthusiastic and powerful faith. And indeed we have only to listen to Ben Sirach speak of Israel's Wisdom: "Wisdom will praise herself, and will glory in the midst of her people. In the assembly of the Most High she will open her mouth" (24, 1-2).

For what foreign culture would Israel exchange this Wisdom, and this one boasted of being the culture of the whole of humanity?

Moreover, is Israel master of this Wisdom? Is it up to Israel to dispose of her since it did not choose her, but she came and established herself in Israel? To show this supremacy Ben Sirach expresses himself in language rather unusual for his customary way of expressing himself:

"In the waves of the sea, in the whole earth, and in every people and nation I have gotten a possession. Among all these I sought a resting place; I sought in whose territory I might lodge. Then the Creator of all things gave me a commandment, and the one who created me assigned a place for my tent. And he said, 'Make your dwelling in Jacob, and in Israel receive your inheritance.'

"From eternity, in the beginning, he created me, and from eternity I shall not cease to exist. In the holy tabernacle I ministered before him, and so I was established in Zion. In the beloved city likewise he gave me a resting place, and in Jerusalem was my dominion. So I took root in an honored people, in the portion of the Lord, who is their inheritance" (24, 6-12).

Such a Wisdom was not likely to allow herself to be drawn into any culture whatsoever. Though all Asia was ready to accept a vast religious and spiritual syncretism, Israel's Wisdom was not able to compromise herself without renouncing herself.

If she imposes herself invincibly upon Israel, it is because she has issued from the mouth of God: "He has ordained the splendors of his divine wisdom, and he is from everlasting to everlasting. Nothing can be added or token away, and he needs no one to be his counselor" (42, 21).

Men, in fact, have not in any way taken part in building her up; and if they enjoy her it is because the Lord has granted her as a free gift to whomever he pleases:

"All wisdom comes from the Lord and is with him for ever. The sand of the sea, the drops of rain, and the days of eternity, who can count them? The height of heaven, the breadth of the earth, the abyss, and wisdom, who can search them out?

"Wisdom was created before all things, and prudent understanding from eternity. The root of wisdom, to whom has it been revealed? Her clever devices, who knows them? There is one who is wise, greatly to be feared, sitting upon his throne. The Lord himself created wisdom; he saw her and apportioned her, he poured her out upon all his works. She dwells with all flesh according to his gift, and he supplied her to those who love him" (1, 1-10).

Through her very origin the Wisdom of Israel remains irreducible to every tradition and to anything the world regards as extremely valuable.

Judging by external appearances, the disciple of this Wisdom resembles all other sages. Like them he observes and meditates; like them he enriches his experience through contact with the ancients, with men reputed for their knowledge and prudence, with people whom he meets in the course of his travels. But where he greatly differs from other sages is that his study is not pursued with the sole aid of his perspicacity and understanding. He awaits light from God alone:

"He will preserve the discourse of notable men and penetrate the subtleties of parables; he will seek out the hidden meanings of proverbs and be at home with the obscurities of parables. He will serve among great men and appear before rulers; he will travel through lands of foreign nations, for he tests the good and evil among men. He will set his heart to rise early to seek the Lord who made him, and will make supplication before the Most High; he will open his mouth in prayer and make supplication for his sins. If the great Lord is willing, he will be filled with the spirit of understanding" (39, 2-6).

The effort at personal reflection, required of all who seek the truth, is not sufficient: the sage of Israel must, first and above all, be ready to receive, maintain himself perfectly disposable, be at the call of a Word from eternity, whether he received it directly or it was transmitted to him, and he must guard this word jealously in his heart as the greatest of treasures:

"Be ready to listen to every narrative, and do not let wise proverbs escape you. If you see an intelligent man, visit him early; let your foot wear out his doorstep. Reflect on the statutes of the Lord, and meditate at all times on his commandments. It is he who will give insight to your mind, and your desire for wisdom will be granted" (6, 35-37).

This is exactly what sets the Jews apart from others and prevents them from freely accepting every culture, a fortiori of allowing themselves to be assimilated by that culture. They agree to share in a common search for human truth as long as there would always be in them an area of thought which would remain impenetrable, because they are not its masters: a superior will reigns there and their wisdom consists in submitting to this will: "If you desire wisdom, keep the commandments!" (1, 26). "All wisdom is fear of the Lord, and in all wisdom there is the fulfillment of the law" (19, 20).

When Ben Sirach encourages his disciples to observe the Law, he does this with such insistence that we may ask whether he intends to identify the Law with Wisdom: "All this is the book of the covenant of the Most High, the law which Moses commanded us as an inheritance for the congregations of Jacob. It fills men with wisdom, like the Pishon and like the Tigris at the time of the first fruits" (24, 23-25).

It is natural that all gather round the Torah at a time when Judaism, conscious of what threatens it, is on the alert. They will prove their fidelity to their national Wisdom by conforming their conduct to the Mosaic Law. However, we have here much more than simply the attachment of a people to its ancestral customs. The Israelite's love of the Law lies in his seeing in this law the love of the God who chose him. Obedience to the minutiae of the law is witnessing to a world which has no analogue in the human order.

Judaism will put a stop to all outside pressures; it will escape the powerful movement which carries humanity along in its search for political and spiritual unity. As the Chosen One of God, Israel cannot allow itself to be swallowed up in the mass of peoples led on by only a human knowledge. Rather it will resign itself to live on the periphery of these nations, misunderstood, despised and hated, as though not of the same race of men. The world, after making the attempt at reducing it through persuasion and violence, will finally have to bear with it as a neighbor and accept it as it is.

◦　◦　◦

The world, having failed in bringing about unity, is forced to admit this strange and irritating duality. However, Judaism does not accept the fact that there can be two worlds, for it well knows there is only one true Wisdom, and that she presided over the whole creation. She is equally good for all humanity in general.

This Wisdom reigned over all nations from the beginning: "He made for them tongue and eyes; he gave them ears and a mind for thinking. He filled them with knowledge and understanding, and showed them good and evil. He set his eyes upon their hearts to show them the majesty of his works" (17, 6-8).

However, when sin invaded the world, Wisdom retreated little by little, finding it impossible to discover a resting place in the world (cf. 24, 7), until the day when she set up her tent in Israel,* which retained the privilege of her presence in spite of past failures, for "Israel is the Lord's own portion" (17, 17).

Even though Wisdom's empire has been greatly diminished, nothing prevents her from being destined for all, since all have received like Israel enough light to contemplate and praise their

---

* Ben Sirach seems to speak here of the Sect of the **New Alliance,** brought to light by the Dead Sea Scrolls. He gives high praise to Simon II's family, the father of Onias III. Some say this Onias is the Teacher of Righteousness of the Qumran writings. We should not think it was only by chance that the Hebrew text of Ecclesiasticus was found in the genizah of the Old Cairo Synagogue, along with the so-called Damascus Document and the Zadokite Fragment.

Creator and the splendor of creation. Yahweh who has bestowed life upon all has also granted them a Covenant which will not pass away: "He established with them an eternal covenant, and showed them his judgments. Their eyes saw his glorious majesty, and their ears heard the glory of his voice. And he said to them, 'Beware of all unrighteousness.' And he gave commandment to each of them concerning his neighbor" (17, 12-14).

Most people were oblivious of this Covenant, but Israel, while waiting for them to find the road once more, stands up in their midst as the witness of God's universal love: "The compassion of man is for his neighbor, but the compassion of the Lord is for all living beings. He rebukes and trains and teaches them, and turns them back, as a shepherd his flock" (18, 13).

Better still, Israel stands before God as the rough draft of humanity, of a humanity which has chosen to follow God's will when faced with the decision of acceptance or refusal: "What race is worthy of honor? The human race. What race is worthy of honor? Those who fear the Lord. What race is unworthy of honor? Those who transgress the commandments" (10, 19).

Ben Sirach seemingly goes that far: since the Law alone can give life, no one is free from following it. True, Israel alone fully knows the Law, but all are under its jurisdiction. The idea will be taken up more explicitly in the Book of Wisdom, but here we see its outline: "Before a man are life and death, and whichever he chooses will be given to him. For great is the wisdom of the Lord; he is mighty in power and sees everything; his eyes are on those who fear him, and he knows every deed of man. He has not commanded any man to be ungodly, and he has not given anyone permission to sin" (15, 17-20).

Passing in the eyes of others for an essentially heterogeneous and irreducible race, Israel believes iteslf to be linked to the rest of humanity. Though it has no right to exchange its Wisdom with any other human wisdom constructed by the human spirit, it feels that all men sooner or later will be called upon to live according to this transcendent Wisdom and obey her laws. Israel answers the pretentions to universalism of the philosophies of higher civilizations with the claim of a universalism powerful in another way, viz., the commandments of God.

Israel for the moment is the only possessor of this superior Wisdom. Here we have an anomaly which could not escape Ben Sirach. He attempts to explain it through the oppositions he observes in nature. As creation is perfect, he gladly undertakes its defense:

"Why is any day better than another, when all the daylight in the year is from the sun? By the Lord's decision they were distinguished, and he appointed the different seasons and feasts; some of them he exalted and hallowed, and some of them he made ordinary days. All men are from the ground, and Adam was created from the dust. In the fullness of his knowledge the Lord distinguished them and appointed their different ways; some of them he blessed and exalted, and some of them he made holy and brought near himself; but some of them he cursed and brought low, and turned them out of their place. As clay in the hands of the potter, for all his ways are as he pleases, so men are in the hand of him who made them, to give them as he decides. Good is the opposite of evil, and life the opposite of death; so the sinner is the opposite of the godly. Look upon all the works of the Most High; they likewise are in pairs, one the opposite of the other" (33, 7-15).

This is evidently a narrow point of view. Though it gives assurance to Ben Sirach's optimism, we may think the contrasts he observes are not necessarily the work of God; that evil will be removed and the sinner converted; that the Jews one day will meet with the Gentiles to commune in the same truth, the unity and universality of which Ben Sirach so well states.

✿ ✿ ✿

This, however, is not the immediate problem presented to

Ben Sirach, and it matters little if he has given a somewhat unsafe solution.

Although it is true that history tends to unity in spite of the divisiveness contrary to this unity, still it is not by a denial of their Election that the Jews could allow this law to take its course. Rather they should work, as will the Christians, to share their privilege with the rest of the world. This unity will be effected neither by the great empires nor by human ideologies, but it will be brought about in proportion to the way in which the universal call of the God of Sinai is heard. Abandoned to himself, man is capable only of building towers of Babel. Destined to remain incomplete, these towers resemble ruins even before they become ruins.

Ben Sirach deserves credit for strengthening Israel against the incontestable prestige of Hellenism. Israel will draw anything which will enrich its patrimony from Hellenism, but it will not alienate anything from its patrimony in doing so. Thanks to Ben Sirach, the Chosen People, refusing to co-operate in the building of passing dreams, will remain faithful to a Wisdom whose secret the world will never learn. It will remain faithful also to its destiny as the guiding People.

On this condition the Cross of Christ will be able to reconcile Israel with the universe from which it seemed to be irremediably cut off: "For he is our peace, who has made us both one, and has broken down the dividing wall of hostility, by abolishing in his flesh the law of commandments and ordinances, that he might create in himself one new man in place of the two, so making peace, and might reconcile us both to God in one body through the cross, thereby bringing the hostility to an end" (Eph. 2, 14-16).

C.- BEN SIRACH'S OPTIMISM

The impending struggle allowed neither doubts nor hesitations. He is already half defeated who is not sure of the excellence of his cause nor of the victory. Israel was to march to the combat with an invincible assurance, with an intrepid faith in the religious values it was to uphold.

Also, Wisdom, whose herald Ben Sirach is, presents herself with an optimism fit to bolster one's spirits: can anything but good come to one who abandons himself to the Hand of God? The sage is so persuaded of this truth that he intones his act of thanksgiving in advance.

✦   ✦   ✦

He sets up a kind of *synthesis of the teaching and the spirituality of Israel.*

The idea may seem a bit premature, for certain problems still remain without a solution. But it answered the needs of the hour so well that it had to be retained and used in every possible way. How, in fact, allow minds to question themselves on so many essential questions? Man needs certitude especially when he has to make his own decisions.

And that is why, in his very imperfect vision of the divine plan, Ben Sirach sings of the harmony of creation which, thanks to God, has finally become conscious of the fullness of its destiny.

✦   ✦   ✦

First, the lot of man is in the hands of an all-powerful God, whose will is opposed to the vain grandeurs of the world. Is it not from this theological postulate that every effort of biblical reflection is born? "The government of the earth is in the hands of the Lord. . . . The beginning of man's pride is to depart from the Lord" (10, 4, 12).

The master of the universe is not a disdainful and distant potentate. Though he smashes the disobedience of the proud, he watches solicitously over the humble: "The Lord has cast down the thrones of rulers, and has seated the lowly in their places" (10, 14). "The prayer of the poor man goes from his lips to the ears of God" (21, 5).

Man can confide in God alone: "Let us fall into the hands of the Lord, but not into the hands of men; for as his majesty is, so also is his mercy" (2, 18).

Undoubtedly the sage will have recourse to human means without any scruple when there is need. When he is sick, for example, he will not refuse the aid of a doctor (38, 12), for does not God place them at our disposal? In the final analysis, it is abandonment to his will which is the condition and secret of happiness:

"He who trusts in the Lord will not suffer loss" (32, 24). "No evil will befall the man who fears the Lord, but in trial he will deliver him again and again" (33, 1). "There is no loss in the fear of the Lord, and with it there is no need to seek help" (40, 26).

Ben Sirach speaks of this from his own experience: "I have often been in danger of death, but have escaped because of these experiences. The spirit of those who fear the Lord will live, for their hope is in him who saves them" (34, 12-13).

Abandon oneself to God? Certainly. But to what does this lead the just man? It leads to salvation, to life, and to the possession of all things. What will this salvation, life, and satiety be made up of? Job and Qoheleth had doubted the happiness of the just too much, and Ben Sirach maintains a prudent reserve on the point. From all the evidence, Wisdom baffles our intelligence by the way she leads us: "For at first she will walk with him in tortuous paths, she will bring fear and cowardice upon him, and torment him by her discipline until she trust him, and she will test him with her ordinances" (4, 17). The just man is not sheltered from trials; from them he will be formed in patience: "My son, if you come forward to serve the Lord, prepare yourself for temptation. Set your heart right and be steadfast, and do not be hasty in time of calamity. Cleave to him and do not depart, that you may be honored at the end of your life. Accept whatever is brought upon you, and in changes that humble you be patient" (2, 1-4).

It is not a question of escaping the present, for there would be only delusion in speculating upon the future to console oneself for the suffering one is undergoing: "A man of no understanding has vain and false hopes, and dreams give wings to fools" (34, 1).

The future is barred by death, the unavoidable necessity of which one is better off to accept: ". . . this is the decree of the Lord for all flesh, and how can you reject the good pleasure of the Most High?" (41, 4).

We should not demand, here and now, from life more than it can give us.

First, though reasons for sadness abound in the world, it is healthy psychology not to dwell too much on them: "Do not give yourself over to sorrow, and do not afflict yourself deliberately. . . . Delight your soul and comfort your heart, and remove sorrow far from you, for sorrow has destroyed many, and there is no profit in it" (30, 21, 23).

The dead themselves, though worthy of honor and tears, should not be mourned beyond "one or two days": we must do what we should, but it would be foolish to afflict ourselves too much with what cannot be remedied: "Do not forget, there is no coming back; you do the dead no good, and you injure yourself" (38, 21).

Again, the best way not to suffer is to avoid throwing oneself deliberately in its path; one must know how to control one's ambitions, to be content with one's task and condition, and not to attempt anything out of the ordinary: "Seek not what is too difficult for you, nor investigate what is beyond your power. Reflect upon what has been assigned to you, for you do not need what is hidden. Do not meddle in what is beyond your tasks, for matters too great for human understanding have been shown you" (3, 21-23).

Finally, why not enjoy and even seek out the happiness that is within our reach? "Do not deprive yourself of a happy day; let not your share of desired good pass by you" (14, 14).

How would happiness not find its place also in a perfect world in which ". . . it is not possible to diminish or increase them"? (18, 6).

Everything in this world has its place, fixed by eternal Wisdom: "The works of the Lord have existed from the beginning by his creation, and when he made them, he determined their divisions. He arranged his works in an eternal order, and their dominion for all generations; they neither hunger nor grow weary, and they do not cease from their labors. They do not crowd one another aside, and they never disobey his word" (16, 26-28).

Everything in the world travels towards its goal in a harmonious way: "Because of God his messenger finds his way, and by his word all things hold together" (43, 26).

Can one doubt that all, even when we cannot understand it, is not disposed according to our needs? "The works of the Lord are all good, and he will supply every need in its hour. And no one can say, 'This is worse than that,' for all things will prove good in their season" (39, 33-34).

Everything has its *raison d'etre*. Everything is useful and good, even the co-existence of good and evil: "One confirms the good things of the other" (42, 25).

We cannot be too optimistic. In Sirach's way of life nothing should be allowed to spoil our joy. Joy is the only atmosphere in which man can develop; it is the condition of life and even life itself: "Gladness of heart is the life of man, and the rejoicing of a man is length of days" (30, 22).

This is true because happiness springs from God as its source: "The fear of the Lord delights the heart, and gives gladness and joy and long life" (1, 12).

Ben Sirach has too realistic a sense of life for the present moment not to appear to him as the only one that belongs to man. If there is a moment in which to repair the past, or to prepare for the future, it is the present moment. While Ben Sirach enriches it with this joy of life which will give him such remarkable dynamism, nevertheless the lesson of Qoheleth has not been lost.

Sirach does not confine himself, however, so closely in this preoccupation with the present moment as did his predecessor. His aspirations goes beyond this moment and he looks out into the future. His glance is not heavy and dull, and he is able to see nothing but good in the future. This is a result of his optimism. He does not avoid the irritating problem of retribution which was considered in his attempt at a synthesis.

God's justice must not be called into question. Though late in coming, it will come in its good time: "With him who fears the Lord it will go well in the end; on the day of his death he will be blessed" (1, 13).

The sage must guard against all impatience. He receives example for this from on high: ". . . for the Lord is slow to anger" (5, 4).

The wait will be long perhaps, but man will receive his due in the end: "For it is easy in the sight of the Lord to reward a man on the day of his death according to his conduct. The misery of an hour makes one forget luxury, and at the close of a man's life his deeds will be revealed. Call no one happy before his death; a man will be known through his children" (11, 26-28).

              ❊   ❊   ❊

Ben Sirach had recourse to this final manifestation of God's justice in order to patch up the fault which the poem of Job and Ecclesiastes had believed to be present in God's work. His explanation seems somewhat weak. But could a better one be found when Jewish doctrine had not yet discovered the extra-temporal dimension of human destiny? Was it not praiseworthy to seek a way out of the impasse, after the failure of the traditional solutions? Even though the solution he presents is rather inexact, his intuition is nonetheless good.

Should we reproach Ben Sirach for too excessive an optimism and too exaggerated a faith? He quickly patches up certain cracks that run through the granite of his walls. He justifies the presence of evil, the existence of the Gentiles, the reward of the good and the bad. As weak as are the explanation which satisfy him, he knows and would have one believe that the edifice in which Israel is going to entrench itself is unshakable. This is not the hour for speculation, but for certitude.

His optimism answers a demand of his own nature; it presupposes an undeniable dose of good will and courage, and a strong good sense which preserves his vitality intact.

❖   ❖   ❖

In any case, it does have a very happy consequence: in a universe which presents no problems to him, it is lawful for Ben Sirach to have this Wisdom come down again, which Job and especially Qoheleth sought for in vain (24, 7-8).

At the same time Sirach finally discovers that *perfect woman,* modeled after the image of Wisdom, whom Qoheleth had despaired of ever encountering: "Children and the building of a city establish a man's name, but a blameless wife is accounted better than both" (40, 19).

Woman, without a doubt, had an unfortunate role to play and can still be the source of many evils: "From a woman sin had its beginning, and because of her all die" (25, 24). "Any iniquity is insignificant compared to a wife's iniquity" (25, 19).

But in this world a wife can assure her husband of three things, viz., peace, joy, and life:

"Happy is the husband of a good wife; the number of his days will be doubled. A loyal wife rejoices her husband, and he will complete his years in peace. A good wife is a great blessing;

she will be granted among the blessings of a man who fears the Lord. Whether rich or poor, his heart is glad, and at times his face is cheerful" (26, 1-4).

Wisdom and Woman, these two closely associated themes in Proverbs, have at last found their place on earth, in spite of Job and Ecclesiastes. Human nature has nothing more to desire.

❊  ❊  ❊

So perfect is Ben Sirach's satisfaction that there remains nothing more to do than intone his hymn of *thanksgiving*. This thanksgiving is more than simply cries of happiness. It is an effusion of gratitude which must climb to the throne of the Creator from the creature: "He set his eye upon their hearts, to show them the majesty of his works" (17, 8).

Is it not for the sake of serving in "the holy tent" in the presence of the Most High that Wisdom has entered "into the inheritance of Israel"? (24, 8). What makes up David's greatness is not his having founded a kingdom and a dynasty, but rather his rendering homage to Yahweh: "In all that he did he gave thanks to the Holy One, the Most High, with ascriptions of glory; he sang praise with all his heart, and he loved his Maker" (47, 8).

To praise the Lord is the sublime function of the living: "Who will sing praises to the Most High in Hades, as do those who are alive and give thanks? From the dead, as from one who does not exist, thanksgiving has ceased; he who is alive and well sings the Lord's praise" (17, 27-28).

Ben Sirach will take care not to fail in this duty: "And for these things bless him who made you, and satisfies you with his good gifts" (32, 13).

Should we be surprised at his attachment to the liturgy of the Temple? Among the many great figures he speaks about (cf. 44-50), there are none he more willingly dwells on than that of Aaron, on whom Yahweh had conferred the priesthood of the people and whom he invested "with perfect glory" (45, 6-22); he speaks also of the high priest Simon (50, 1-21), whose majesty enchants him: "How glorious he was when the people gathered round him. . . . Finishing the service at the altars, and arranging the offering of the Most High, the Almighty" (50, 5, 14).

Though Sirach is pleased to depict the pomp of the ceremonies, it is not because he is interested in any stilted ritualism or narrow formalism: in his eyes the liturgy must be the expansion of an *interior joy* which is inseparable from a life *without blame*: "To keep from wickedness is pleasing to the Lord . . . and to forsake unrighteousness is atonement. . . . The offering of a righteous man anoints the altar. . . . With every gift show a cheerful face" (35, 3, 6, 9).

On this condition the warm and triumphant hymn to which Ben Sirach invites faithful souls will be able to resound legitimately to the praise of the living God: "So now sing praise with all your heart and voice, and bless the name of the Lord" (39, 35). "When you praise the Lord, exalt him as much as you can; for he will surpass even that. When you exalt him, put forth all your strength, and do not grow weary, for you cannot praise him enough" (43, 30).

Infinite is the glory of the Most High and the sages will not fail to share in it, as their predecessors did: "People will declare their wisdom, and the congregation proclaims their praise" (44, 15; cf. 39, 10).

Should we not see this as a reward to the just man which is guaranteed at his last hour? "His memory will not disappear, and his name will live through all generations. . . . If he lives long, he will leave a name greater than a thousand, and if he goes to rest, it is enough for him" (39, 9, 11).

The divine work will not end in defeat, but in victory, and this calls for thanksgiving.

And here is the final lesson of the synthesis of Jewish spirituality which the sage proposes to those who will have to be on the defensive against the threats of Hellenism. It calls to mind the triumphant "Amen" of the Apocalypse.

❊   ❊   ❊

In short, it is not by surrendering to a morbid need of self-criticism, accusing itself of its failures, that Judaism, and later on Christianity, will draw attention, admiration, and the respect of the world. Both can and must give evidence of one and the same thing: a clear consciousness of the riches they possess; a real joy through which they express their gratitude; and an unshakable faith in the happy outcome of a destiny which is in the hands of God.

# THE BOOK OF DANIEL

5 The Book of Daniel, placed by the Jewish Bible among the "other writings," has been attached to the series of the great prophets in the christian tradition. This is undoubtedly because of its messianic importance.

If we eliminate the 18th and 19th chapters, additions written later on in Greek, the work is comprised of two parts containing six chapters in each part. The first part is *narrative* and deals with six episodes, the heroes of which are Daniel and his companions in the Exile. The second part is *apocalyptic* and presents four "visions," one written in Aramaic and the other three in Hebrew. We still feel the work is that of the same author even though these two parts are two very different literary genres.

The author (and this is the opinion of many exegetes, even Catholic) could have written the work after the profanation of the Temple at Jerusalem by Antiochus Epiphanes (December, 167), or after the first Maccabean successes; in any case, before June, 164. The sacred writer, moved by the sufferings of the Jews anxiously asking when their trial would end, set himself the task of consoling and encouraging them.

Between the assassination of the high priest Onias III in 171, which marked the commencement of the persecution, and the sacrilege of 167, there was a period of three and one half years, a half-week of years. This proved to be a ray of light for the author of Daniel. Referring to the seventy weeks of servitude predicted by Jeremiah (Jer. 29, 10), he calculated that the end of the trial had come. In the violence of the Seleucid era he saw clearly the final assault of the nations against Israel which would precede the definitive thriumph of the saints. This appears to be the general meaning of the "visions."

As for the *narratives*, these have as their purpose the comforting of the victims of Antiochus. They had probably been told over a long period of time. They could have consisted of a cycle of folklore centered on Daniel. The author perhaps collected these and adapted them to his plan; he preserved their legendary character which is not always in accord with true history.

A number of Catholic exegetes is far from agreeing with this thesis. They are reluctant to admit that the canon of the Scriptures can include this pseudepigraphic genre of apocalypses. Also, they do not want to allow one of the Bible's most popular prophets to lose his historical authority.

We are sympathetic to the arguments used in its defense and accept this thesis. We do this all the more willingly since the Book of Daniel appears to take on the spiritual meaning which we believe it is supposed to convey simply because of this thesis.

A.- THE TRIAL OF FIDELITY

At the time when Jeremiah announced the advent of the New Covenant which was to be sealed in the heart of each individual among the Elect, it seemed as though this Covenant was imminent. However, there remained much time for preparing these hearts to receive the divine call and for enlightening, guiding, and strengthening their fidelity. And this was the explicit mission of Jewish Wisdom.

It is easy, when looking back, to pass severe judgment upon the People for their slowness to understand and their discouragement which seemed always to be on the verge of springing up.

After all, this People had been constantly instructed, reassured, and encouraged by the "witnesses of God." However, in the apparent obscurity in which the human actors of this drama were fighting who would not, without some special· enlightenment, have at least been tempted to question the real meaning of the Election?

In spite of Ben Sirach's desire to explain everything, this darkness, which had caused so much anguish to Job and so much sadness to Qoheleth, was not dissipated. It is because it was to be the crucible in which the Jewish soul was purified and its fidelity tried. Unless this took place the great plan of God could not be realized.

The disappointing circumstances of the Return, the diminishment of the Jewish state, now reduced to the smallest in the immense Persian empire, the dangerous position of the just, all these things were of such a nature as to shake the assurance of the best.

A new difficulty was going to arise from Alexander's victories: Hellenism, in its desire to unify its conquests, was not able to tolerate the resistance of a People singularized by the observance of a Law which was judged to be both unintelligible and unassimilable. Would it not be forced to break this people since it was unable to bend them? Antiochus Epiphanes will act like Alexander. Unable to untie the Gordion knot, he cut it with his sword.

The just, then, will have to prove their fidelity. They will have to overcome their doubts in a promise so frequently held back by delays, and they will be forced to stand up to the hostility of a world no longer anxious to rule over territories but over minds. The Jew will undergo the pressure of governments resolved to impose on him the discipline of their teaching and their culture. He will be reproached for his faith and even persecuted for it. The trial will be from without the within. To uphold the privilege of his Election he will have to fight against the world and himself.

This will be a difficult struggle, but its still unforeseeable outcome will make a victorious Israel take a great stride forward on the road to its destiny.

Also, if God demands of his Elect so heroic a witness and so unconditional a commitment that their confidence in him is abandoned blindly to his will, then it cannot be without good reason. When he asks them to surrender even their life as proof of their attachment, is he not making it understood that his Hand can protect one beyond the portals of death?

The persecution of Antiochus Epipanes will open to the Jewish mind the immensity of unknown horizons. After almost two centuries of suffering, the Jew longed for and awaited this. Israel now is on the point of discovering the dimension of human existence which lies beyond the limits of this world.

*　*　*

To face up to the dangers of totalitarian Hellenism, Israel's Wisdom had felt the need of becoming more fully conscious of herself and laying claim to an unequalled superiority over all others. The salutary reaction of Ben Sirach could have been understood and shared with only a small select group. Their ideas had hardly a chance to influence the minds of the humble classes, and these latter also had to make their own decisions. The humbler classes, as we know, are more moved by the eloquence of simple pictures than by the power of reasoning.

Throughout the third century we see the development of a folklore which is fed by edifying examples of pious Jews who lived according to the Law of Moses under the worst circumstances.

The edifying stories told of these pious Jews have as background a period of time made sacred through legend. The sadness and horror of the historic content of this period is toned down. Greek domination, endured at present, made it possible for people to recall the Persian rule without any feelings of repugnance. Even the Babylonian potentates seemed almost debonair who viewed through the prism of legend. In order to condemn the actual rulers, these stories presented Nebuchadnezzar as an understanding and a benevolent ruler, without any recollection of his haughty attitude.

And so we have the cycle of Daniel and his companions who were honored at the Babylonian court. It fills the chapters of the book such as we know it.

The young Jews hardly appeared before Nebuchadnezzar when the latter entrusts them high offices: "Then the king gave Daniel high honors and many gifts, and made him ruler over the whole province of Babylon, and chief prefect over all the wise men of Babylon. Daniel made request of the king, and he appointed Shadrach, Meshach, and Abednego over the affairs of the prince of Babylon; but Daniel remained at the king's court" (22, 48-49).

Darius, the Mede, successor of Belshazzar after his death, far from withdrawing such exceptional favors from Daniel, made him one of the three ministers charged with controlling the one hundred and twenty satraps who administered the kingdom in his name.

"Then this Daniel became distinguished above all other presidents and satraps, because an excellent spirit was in him; and the king planned to set him over the whole kingdom" (6, 3).

The idea described here will be used by christian apologetics: the State will never find more worthy ministers than the servants of God!

The satraps and ministers were offended at the influence of the sons of Israel because of their zeal and intelligence. Perhaps, because of their shrewdness! They worked hard to ruin this influence. Their ill-will, however, could never catch their rivals in any fault. "But they could find no ground for complaint or any fault, because he was faithful, and no error or fault was found in him" (6, 4).

As a last resource they found fault with their belief: "Then these men said, 'We shall not find any ground for complaint against this Daniel unless we find it in connection with the law of his God' " (6, 5).

This was a marvelous discovery. Henceforth, this will be the unpardonable crime in the eyes of the world, the only accusation it can make against the Jews, and later on against the Christians! They will be the most fiercely persecuted by those whom they embarrass.

Must we add that this accusation is far from being ineffectual? One differs from the world in matters of morals and religion at his own risk. The Israelites were not long in learning this. While they wait to be cast to the lions or into the furnace, their fidelity to the Law of Moses exposes them to many sufferings.

However, God, in whom the just place their trust, can deliver them from every evil. We shall learn that Belteshazzar, Shadrach, Meshach, and Abednego (so called by the chief eunuch), in spite of the ten days of privations they endured rather than *"defile themselves with the king's rich food, or with the wine which he drank . . . they were better in appearance and fatter in flesh than all the youths who ate the king's rich food"* (1, 15).

Cannot God draw his friends from the most difficult positions, even the most desperate, without any harm to them? With him there is nothing to fear: neither the water which engulfs one (Ps, 66, 6; Is. 43, 2), nor a consuming fire (Ps. 57, 5;; Ps. 91, 13). One should face fearlessly the "trial of fidelity," just as the three young Jews: "If it be so, our God whom we serve is able to deliver us from the burning fiery furnace; and he will deliver us out of your hand, O King" (2, 17).

Were this protection denied to him, the servant of God would still brave the torments rather than deny his faith: "But if not, be it known to you, O King, that we will not serve your gods or worship the golden image which you have set up" (3, 18).

God cannot betray a confidence such as this. He will uphold it before a world so sure of itself: Hananiah, Mishael, and Azariah will come forth from the furnace unscathed, while the

Chaldeans will be devoured by its flames. Nebuchadnezzar will have to admit he is not master of the universe:

"Blessed be the God of Shadrach, Meshash, and Abednego, who has sent his angel and delivered his servants, who trusted in him, and set at naught the king's command, and yielded up their bodies rather than serve and worship any god except their own God" (3, 28).

The aged Darius offers the same homage when he hastens to the den of the lions and cries out: "O Daniel, servant of the living God, has your God, whom you serve continually, been able to deliver you from the lions?" (6, 21).

God's children, who rely only on the Lord for salvation, come forth victors from the trial. When one persecutes them, he defies God himself; this defiance finally turns against the persecutors, for his own glory which shines out in the eyes of the world and for the glory of his followers whom he judges it right to put on trial.

*     *     *

The Jews, when reading these stories, grew accustomed to the notion that fidelity to the Law was the touchstone of their faith; for them, the suffering Servant whose figure stands out in Isaiah's message was the type offered every true Israelite.

But they are still far from understanding this trial; they did not know how far God would permit it to go. The beautiful and elevating stories contained in Daniel were re-assuring: how could the heroes in the drama of faith fail to be victorious when God would take their fate into his own hands?

The events of 168-167 will shock this simple optimism.

Onias III, Jerusalem's high priest, and brother of the same Simon whom Sirach praised, is despoiled of his pontificate by his brother Jason.

The latter succeeds him in office. Immediately: "Jason at once shifted his countrymen over to the Greek way of life. . . . He destroyed the lawful ways of living and introduces new customs contrary to the law. . . . There was such an extreme of Hellenism and such an increase in the adoption of foreign ways because of the surpassing wickedness of Jason, who was ungodly and no high priest, that the priests were no longer intent upon their service at the altar . . . despising the sanctuary and neglecting the sacrifices . . ." (2 Mac. 4, 10-14).

The practice of the Law is forbidden, especially prescriptions relative to circumcision and the Sabbath. Renegades, supported by the Seleucids, concentrate upon one section of the city in order to live more freely according to Greek ways. Everywhere, at the crossroads, the public squares, in villages and in woods, they multiply their places of worship and offer sacrifice to Artemis and Aphrodite, to Hermas and Hecate, to the nymphs, and to Pan. Worse still: the Temple is profaned; Temple slaves and prostitutes were seen there in large numbers; forbidden meat was eaten there to the sound of instruments and during sacrilegious dances. Impiety reached its highest pitch the day the altar was used to honor Olympian Zeus. The date of 15 Caslew, 145, in the Seleucid era (8th of December, 167), owes its frightful celebrity to these horrors.

Judaism seemed forever crushed. Deep was the grief of the Jews who remained faithful. They could not understand how their God, the living God, remained silent when provoked and insulted in his own sanctuary. He seemed either indifferent or powerless to stop it. Apostasy was triumphant. Anyone who resisted would pay with his own life.

In several places, Daniel brings out the dark role to be played by Antiochus, the "little horn": ". . . with a mouth speaking great things" (7, 8).

He will speak, think, and act: "He shall speak words against the Most High, and shall wear out the saints of the Most High, and shall think to change the times and the law; and they shall be given into his hand . . ." (7, 25). "And on the wing of the Temple will be the disastrous abomination" (9, 27).

This is a repetition, it seems, of the 587 catastrophe: ". . . and the people of the prince who is to come shall destroy the city and the sanctuary. Its end shall come with a flood, and to the end shall be war; desolations are decreed" (9, 26).

But much worse is today's misfortune: in the sixth century it was a guilty Israel that Nebuchadnezzar, the scourge of God, was given the mission to punish; now, for injustice, crime, and apostasy, there is no punishment; for the saints, persecution, death and ruin: "As I looked this horn made war on the saints, and prevailed over them . . ." (7, 21). "A king of bold countenance, shall cause fearful destruction, and shall succeed in what he does, and destroy mighty men and the people of the saints" (8, 24).

We must not see in the event the manifestation of the divine wrath. If the faithful people are trampled under foot by the forces of evil, it is because God grants them a final respite. Daniel announces the passing character of their crimes: "And from the time that the continual burnt offering is taken away, and the abomination that makes desolate is set up, there shall be a thousand two hundred and ninety days" (12, 11). "The saints shall be given into his hand for a time, two times, and a half time" (7, 25). "When the shattering of the power of the holy people comes to an end all these things shall be accomplished" (12, 7).

The persecution of Epiphanes is then essentially the same as the trial of fidelity to which Daniel and his companions were exposed. Being more radical, however, it would also be more decisive: the outcome of the combat would no longer be the interests or the life of a handful of the faithful, but the salvation of the whole people, and the glorious advent of the New Covenant offered to all.

Judaism is, in fact, placed, in the fulfillment of God's plan, between the Covenant of Sinai, broken since the fall of Jerusalem in 587, and the New Covenant announced by the prophets of the Exile and the advent of which each son of Israel hastens in proportion as he comes out victorious from the trial of fidelity.

Daniel, in fasting and prayer, receives from God a formal assurance of this through the angel Gabriel. He reveals the meaning of the prophecy in which Yahweh predicted Israel's restoration through Jeremiah: "For thus says the Lord, 'When the seventy years are completed for Babylon, I will visit you, and I will fulfill to you my promise and bring you back to this place" (Jer. 29, 10).

These years must be understood as weeks of years. The persecution by Antiochus rages during the period of expiation: "Seventy weeks of years are decreed concerning your people and your holy city, to finish the transgression, to put an end of sin, and to atone for iniquity, to bring in an everlasting righteousness . . ." (9, 24).

Though a high priest (Joshua) rebuilds the temple after the seven first weeks, this is only a short consolation: *"The anguish of times"* will be prolonged still for sixty-two weeks. This is still not salvation, but it is being prepared for in tears and blood.

*       *       *

To be perfect the reparation will impose on Israel the obligation to suffer pain which is its due, but also Israel will have to accept death, like the Servant in the Book of Isaiah. Then God's justice, being satisfied, will manifest itself. As infidelity will lead Israel to death, so fidelity will lead it back to life.

This idea was already *in germ* in the eighth century in Isaiah's message. Imprudently relying on Ashur's power, Ahaz had thrown Judah into a most dangerous situation. The prophet abjures the king to renounce the illusory support of temporal alliances and to utter the one cry that will bring salvation, viz., "Emmanuel," i.e., "Yahweh is with us." This cry is made by neither Ahaz nor Hezekiah. In order for Hezekiah to utter finally this cry, there had to come the terrifying invasion of Sennacherib. Thanks to this resurgence of faith, Israel will see the Assyrian armies recede. Thanks also to the faith and fidelity of the best among them, Israel will be saved from death.

After the angel of the Great Vision said: ". . . many shall run to and fro, and iniquity shall increase . . ." (12, 4), Daniel will recall that a small number of the wise will endure death, but this death will ensure the salvation of Israel: ". . . and some of those who are wise shall fall, to refine and to cleanse them, and to make them white, until the time of the end, for it is yet for the time appointed" (11, 35).

God's hour will not come until his servants, recognizing the futility of human aid, have totally surrendered themselves to his will. This they must do even in the midst of the worst trials, for they are still in his Hands; and even in death itself, from which he is able to deliver them. Only then will God act. Woe to the powerful one of this world who will have dared to stand up proudly against the Prince of princes: ". . . by no human hand he will be broken" (8, 25).

Is not the end of Antiochus evocative of that of Sennacherib? Following his defeat at Pelusium and spurred on by the bad news from the East, the Assyrian had quickly raised the seige of Jerusalem in great rage. Then he went to his shameful death. The Seleucid will fall in the same way because of the places profaned through his wickedness:

"But tidings from the east and the north shall alarm him, and he shall go forth with great fury to exterminate and destroy utterly many. And he shall pitch his palatial tents between the sea and the glorious mountain; yet he shall come to his end, with none to help him" (11, 44-45).

Thus, the crisis of 167, announced by Daniel, found a solution which is within the usual prophetic tradition: the defeat of Judaism is only an illusion; it leads, in reality, to the most astounding victory.

There is no other solution than to endure with patience, which will reach even heroic proportions, the deadly torment, until the moment of divine vengeance.

Many of the Jews, however, even those resolved not to betray their faith, did not grasp this truth.

The followers of the high priest Onias, more directly threatened, undoubtedly sought refuge far from Jerusalem, perhaps at Damascus.* But this flight, through which they thought they were protecting their faith, not only forbade them from then on to celebrate a worship which was illegitimate, but it withdrew them from the Hand of God and compromised his work.

These future Essenes, if it be question of them, will be able to authorize an alliance of their own: they will not be, however, the expected New Israel. They are very much mistaken, as is also the sect of Qumran, about the meaning of the New Covenant: it is the call of God which alone "separates." When he entrenches himself behind his own movement, man deserts. Never has Isaiah, nor Jeremiah, nor Jesus believed it necessary to withdraw from the solidarity that linked them to the sinful People; and it is not dissidents that make up the Church of Christ, but the called.

The initiative is exclusively the Lord's. If God is silent, then each one should remain at his post where he may perhaps have to suffer. But his testimony will give glory to God and service to the people.

Other Jews preferred armed resistance to emigration. They were grouped around the Maccabees.

Their story reminds one of the heroic era of the Conquest and the wars of Yahweh. But have we not yet learned not to confuse

---

* Without entering into the discussion raised by the Qumran Sect, we are tempted to think that the Teacher of Righteousness of the Commentary of Habakkuk is the same one as the high priest Onias III., son of Simon II., whose praise was sung by Sirach.

His pontificate (185-174) ends tragically. Onias was banished and later assassinated in 171. Those remaining faithful to him, denying all legitimacy to all the successors of the high priest, broke off relations with the Temple at Jerusalem and formed the sect of the New Covenant. This was at the beginning of the persecution by Antiochus. From this sect was to come the future Essenes of the christian era.

Yahweh's action with that of Israel's army? Did not Isaiah refuse the co-operation of Hezekiah's troops in order to guarantee the triumph of Yahweh to Zion?

These human means are but a feeble help in a struggle. But who does not feel that these great enterprises draw few real heroes, but many unscrupulous adventurers who are not so much interested in the ideal which inspired the enterprise as the gain they hope to obtain? "And many shall join themselves to them with flattery" (11, 34).

To convince ourselves of this we have only to recall how the adventure undertaken in defense of fidelity will end: the sad history of the Hasmonean dynasty is enough revelation of mediocrity of its spiritual calibre.

Besides, it is not violence that will make a people of saints out of Israel. A decision based on war cannot validly solve the trial of faith imposed on Israel. Nothing will be served by saying that the Hebrews formerly acquired immortal glory by dying on the battle fields of Canaan. Then the future of the nation alone was at stake. Today, in the struggle against Hellenism it is not so much the community which has to conquer as each individual Jew, whose faith must meet the divine demands. God's real soldiers are not men of arms, but the sages and those who will imitate their intrepid abnegation (cf. 11, 33).

Faithful unto death these brave men will take part in the triumph of God, the dispenser and master of life. This life, which springs up endlessly from his bosom, is powerful enough to reanimate and make what was dried up in death flourish once more: "And many of those who sleep in the dust of the earth shall awake, some to everlasting life, and some to shame and everlasting contempt. And those who are wise shall shine like the brightness of the firmament; and those who turn many to righteousness, like the stars for ever and ever" (12, 2-3).

Until now the Bible (only since the Exile and in particular under Ezekiel's pen) had not envisaged any other awakening from death but that of the Chosen People: God having plunged it into death, would recall it to life. But just as this death inflicted on the sinful nation was, as a supreme mark of fidelity, to be accepted by each son of Israel, so the hope of a survival would pass from the collective level to the *personal* level.

The limits of time do not suffice any longer for God to prove his solicitude to the faithful Jews; he raises, now that they are able to understand it, the veil of eternity. And in the Book of Daniel for the first time there shines for the clear, categorical affirmation of a *resurrection* for individuals.

We see how much the era of Judaism, which is a time of trial, contributes to the hastening of the New Covenant and of the definitive reign of justice. Daniel, like all the prophets, undoubtedly does not see beyond his own horizon: this is limited by the events of 167. It is certainly an episode filled with meaning, but it is still only a rough outline of the last act of the divine drama.

Then will appear the Just One who will push obedience to the point of perfection, and this obedience will be as perfect as his holiness and will suffice to atone for the infidelity not only of a generation of his people, but for that of all generations of all races. The sacrifice of the Cross will open up the certitude of the resurrection for all who will associate themselves with it through conformity to the divine model.

B.—THE PEOPLE OF SAINTS AND THE WORLD

The glory of the resurrection, upon which the trial of fidelity will emerge, will be a compensation for the children of Israel; it will hallow their triumph over the forces of evil which are gathered together against them.

It was not that Israel was aggressive by nature. The land which Yahweh had given it was enough. The divine gift is too highly priced for Israel to descend to envying the poor riches of the other nations.

Once attacked, however, Israel is not satisfied with protecting its life and heritage as the possessions of God. It ambitions total victory for the honor of its God. If kings one day enter the City they besiege, it will be as the conquered. They will bear their gifts in unarmed hands and will bow their uncrowned heads in the dust. Punishment will be in proportion to the outrage. Since the universe undertook the assault of Zion, then Israel will dominate the whole universe.

In Daniel's vision the persecution of Antiochus IV will end: "And the kingdom and the dominion and the greatness of the kingdoms under the whole heaven shall be given to the people of the saints of the Most High; their kingdom shall be an everlasting kingdom, and all dominions shall serve and obey them" (7, 27).

The Elect are answerable to God alone. No human power may harm them without divine permission. Yahweh is always the jealous God of Sinai. Even when Israel had experienced the heavy yoke of the conquerors, the Babylonians, the Persians, and the Greeks, it was Yahweh's power and not so much their own that vanquished them. If Nebuchadnezzar's dominion extends so far over the world, it is because Yahweh in his mysterious designs has temporarily delegated this power to him:

"You, O King, the King of Kings, to whom the God of heaven has given the kingdom, the power, and the might, and the glory, and into whose hand he has given, wherever they dwell, the sons of men, the beasts of the field, and the birds of the air, making you rule over them . . ." (2, 37-38).

Later on it is Yahweh who calls Cyrus by name and bids him build Jerusalem and the Temple.

Empires follow. But there is only one king: the God of the Jews, the living God who, like the Orient's god-kings, does not disdain choosing lieutenants to carry out his will on earth: "He changes times and seasons; he removes kings and sets up kings" (2, 21).

Concerning kingdoms, there really is only one; and this belongs to Yahweh. This is what Nebuchadnezzar is forced to admit when he sees the three young Jews coming forth from the furnace: "His kingdom is an everlasting kingdom, and his dominion is from generation to generation" (4, 3).

Darius must also admit this when he sees Daniel come out safely from the den of lions: "For he is a living God, enduring forever; his kingdom shall never be destroyed, and his dominion shall be to the end" (6, 26).

Moreover, the God of Israel is not satisfied with a mere philosophical admission of his sovereignty. When necessary he lets his vicars of the moment feel they are simply exercising a borrowed authority. For when Nebuchadnezzar, contemplating the immensity of his capital from the terrace of his palace, cried out foolishly: "Is not this great Babylon, which I have built by my mighty power as a royal residence and for the glory of my majesty?" (4, 30), from infinity there flashes like a thunderbolt the immediate reply which confirms the interpretation given a year before by Daniel in the dream about the *tree*:

"While the words were still in the king's mouth, there fell a voice from heaven, 'O King Nebuchadnezzar, to you it is spoken: The kingdom has departed from you, and you shall be driven among men, and your dwelling shall be with the beasts of the field; and you shall be made to eat grass like an ox; and seven times shall pass over you, until you have learned that the Most High rules the kingdom of men and gives it to whom he will" (4, 31-32).

It would be a mistake to see here in Israel's teaching a stress on hatred of foreigners. It is simply placing emphasis, and this very calmly, upon the absolute dependence of human powers as far as God is concerned.

It is only when Judaism is threatened that this statement will be tainted with aggressiveness. Yahweh's dominion is then presented as a victory won over the kings of the earth.

For example, in the dream of the *"statue,"* God angrily takes away the authority delegated to his vicars and exercises it himself. Before taking the direction of the world in hand, the Babylonians, the Medes, the Persians, and the Macedonians simply take turns.

Historically this is not entirely exact. The rule of the Medes did not supplant that of the Babylonians since the two powers remained rivals until the day Cyrus united them under his sceptre. But this was a popular version given by the Jews to the unfolding of the events. It was inspired by the Greek way of looking at it: for the Assyrians were substituted the Medes, then the Persians. If Babylon holds the place of Assyria here it is because the Israelites were interested in the world empires insofar as their destiny was involved. The only thing that interested them was to know when they would escape these great political systems which meant to absorb them since the time of Nebuchadnezzar.

The four empires, in which human power seems to perpetuate itself, are symbolized in the Babylonian king's dream by a composite statue made out of metals. These metals are at once increasingly gross and decreasingly pliable, but the last, the hardest, is combined with the friability of clay. Through this symbol, the growing weakness and brutality of the kingdoms is signified. A sudden divine intervention would make the massive structure crumble:

"The head of the image was fine gold and the arms silver, its belly and thighs of bronze, its legs of iron, its feet partly of iron and partly of clay. As you looked, a stone was cut out by no human hand, and it smote the image on its feet of iron and clay, and broke them in pieces; then the iron, the clay, the bronze, the silver, and the gold all together were broken in pieces, and became like the chaff of the summer threshing floors; and the wind carried them away, so that not a trace of them could be found" (2, 32-35).

It is at a time when the rulers of the earth shall have reached the highest peak of pride and despotism that they will be reduced again to nothing, and the true King of the universe will rule without any intermediary:

"And in the days of those kings the God of heaven will set up a kingdom which shall never be destroyed, nor shall its sovereignty be left to another people. It shall break in pieces all these kingdoms and bring them to an end, and it shall stand for ever" (2, 44).

The divine vengeance, provoked by man's insolence, breaks forth at the time when Antiochus IV surpasses all his predecessors in impious audacity: "And at the later end of their rule, when the transgressors have reached their full measure, a king of bold countenance shall arise ... He will rise up even against the Prince of princes; but, by no human hand, he shall be broken" (8, 23, 25).

Making the simple affirmation of God's absolute sovereignty its point of departure, Jewish teaching gradually comes to conceive that, after a decisive struggle, human kingdoms will disappear forever before that of the Most High and his saints.

In the "great beasts that came up out of the sea" (7, 3), which are symbolic of the empires, does there not seem to be a revival of Rahab, Leviathan, Tannin, the legendary monsters which Jahweh had subjugated on the day of Creation? To the victory won by the Creator at the dawn of time there corresponds the victory of the God-King at the end of time.

Concerning the monsters seen by Daniel in his dream, the last and most cruel is about to release his fury over the terror-stricken world when suddenly there arises a Personage whose hoary head gives the appearance of eternity rather than age:

"As I looked, thrones were placed and one that was ancient of days took his seat; his raiment was white as snow, and the hair of his head like pure wool; his throne was fiery flames, its wheels were burning fire. A stream of fire issued and came forth from before him; a thousand thousands served him, and ten thousand times ten thousand stood before him; the court sat in judgment, and the books were opened" (7, 9-10).

The Ancient One who so solemnly comes to occupy his throne to judge the world is none other than he who is before all things, the Alpha and Omega about whom Second Isaiah spoke. He is the Creator outraged by the creature who comes from his hands. Point of departure and end of the universe, he is also that of History: he is the Father of Israel, ally of the persecuted People, whose honor is identified with Yahweh's.

When Belshazzar, presented by Daniel as the son of Nebuchadnezzar, has the vessels of gold and silver taken from the Temple at Jerusalem brought in so that he and his concubines can drink from them, the outrage reaches even to the Most High: "And you his son, Belshazzar, have not humbled your heart, though you knew all this, but you have lifted yourself against the Lord of heaven; and the vessels of his house have been brought in before you, and you and your lords, your wives, and your concubines have drunk wine from them; and you have praised the gods of silver and gold, of bronze, iron, wood, and stone, but the God in whose hand is your breath and whose are all your ways, you have not honored" (5, 22-23).

The same goes for Antiochus IV, for when he will make a criminal attempt upon the holiness of the city and the majesty of the Temple, in persecuting Israel he will be insulting God himself.

God's kingdom is the kingdom of these men whom the world has enslaved for a time. Despised, buffeted, and persecuted like the Servant in the Book of Isaiah, in them God is being offended. And when God takes hold again of the universe, they will share with him the glory of his dominion:

"I saw in the night visions, and behold with the clouds of heaven there came one like the son of man,* and he came to the

---

* In itself the expression "son of man" designates the People of God, as opposed to the kingdoms of the earth. This is apparent when we compare it with the term "people of the saints of the Most High" of verse 18.

It seems, however, that we cannot hold to this primitive meaning: "Without wishing to advance the times and remaining within the perspective of the inspired author, we can ask ourselves whether the Messiah is

154 MAN'S DESTINY IN THE BOOKS OF WISDOM

Ancient of Days and was presented before him. And to him was given dominion and glory and kingdom, that all peoples, nations, and languages should serve him; his dominion is an everlasting dominion, which shall not pass away, and his kingdom one that shall not be destroyed" (7, 13-14).

For this royalty, which has received nothing from the world, has been conferred on the "saints of the Most High" (7, 27); it is nothing else but the kingship of God. And Israel which is identified with him is the stone which, like the rock detached from the mountain side, smashes against the clay of the statue. Nothing will remain of the colossus, not even the dust, for the winds will sweep it away; nothing will remain but this rock which will fill the earth.

"And in days of those kings the God of heaven will set up a kingdom which shall never be destroyed, nor shall its sovereignty be left to another people. It shall break in pieces all these kingdoms and bring them to an end, and it shall stand for ever; just as the stone you saw was cut from the mountain by no human hand, and that it broke in pieces the iron, the bronze, the clay, the silver, and the gold" (2, 44-45).

* * *

Israel was well aware its destiny was out of the ordinary. It also realized that Wisdom precedes in origin the work of creation, that she reigned in the heavens, and that her throne was "in a pillar of cloud" (Eccl. 24, 4).

But this Wisdom appeared until now under the traits of an

---

not included in the vision, or, at least, very close to being included. Just as the four pagan kingdoms are reduced to so many monarchs in verse 17, the People of the Saints perhaps could already be concentrated in one head: the Messiah. Such will be, in any case, the nearest reading made by apocalyptic tradition" (A. Gelin, Dict. de la Bible, Suppl. col. 1201, art. "Messianisme").

Ideal Woman, image of the New Israel: it is she who invites her children to enter a supra-terrestrial world.

Now Wisdom is incarnated in the *"Son of man"*: the mother, it seems, has ceded her place to the children, who enter into God's glory, raised up by the sole power of the Most high.

Heir of the Woman of illustrious origins, the "Son of man" appeared to be identified also with the *Suffering Servant*: the triumph of the one makes one think of the glorification of the other. From one to the other, however, there is a marked difference or, rather, a progression: the Suffering Servant, in whom Israel and its destiny are summed up, is contrasted with the other nations, while the Son of man who abandons himself to God is set in contrast to those who refuse God. In the first case, two ethnic groups are at grips with each other; in the second, two spiritual attitudes.

The distinction, at first sight, may appear forced: to set in contrast Israel and the neighboring nations is the same as confronting Yahweh and the pagan gods, hence two spirits, two ideals, two ways of being religious. In this case, is the Son of man, whom we already recognized in a rudimentary way in the young Jews of the Babylonian court who cry out: "Let it be known, O King, that we will not serve your gods" (3, 18), so different from all those who refused, at the call of the prophets, to adore the Baals?

But, looking at the matter closely, their refusal has an entirely new depth, for it does more than simply reject the food of the gods, the particularism of religions proper to a territory, the cycle-concept of the action of the gods, and their dependence on the will of man who tires to surprise or circumvent their power. Their refusal is to be found in the most intimate depths of the heart; it results from a choice between obedience to God and the pretention of man to govern himself without God.

The pagan religions undoubtedly do nothing else but mask

the worship that man renders to himself. Man, according to Xenophon's observation, creates his gods according to his own image or divinizes his heroes.

❋    ❋    ❋

To sum up, obedience *"usque ad mortem,"* which seemingly reduces the Elect to an irremediable defeat, prepares in reality for the triumph of the resurrection. Those whom the world has wished to eliminate will receive universal empire. God's invincible power exalts the faithful, while it humbles a humanity which, in its Promethean pride, seeks to set its own grandeur over the universe, turning the powers it has received from God to serve its own miserable ends.

One day an eternal Voice will answer violence which aspires, in the name of human viewpoints, to conquer temporal dominion or oppose it, "Put your sword back in its place; for all who take the sword will perish by the sword" (Matt. 26, 52). That same Voice will denounce the emptiness of the proud who believe in the lastingness of the empires they have built up: "My kingship is not of this world; if my kingship were of this world, my servants would fight, that I might not be handed over to the Jews; but my kingship is not from this world" (John 18, 36). Finally, it will announce to the humble the glory of the true kingdom and the joy of acclaiming him who will reign forever: ". . . and you will see the Son of man sitting at the right hand of the Power, and coming with the clouds of heaven" (Mark 14, 62).

C.—WISDOM REVEALS THE MYSTERY OF THE END OF TIME

Wisdom, as depicted in Proverbs, is accessible, welcoming, and helpful: she sets her table for the passer-by, inviting him to find in her everything which promises of the Covenant allow him to hope for.

Her followers soon discover, however, that life reserves for the wise man more anguish than happiness, more grief than joy. When all his happiness was ruined, the holy man Job raised his plaintive cry. Qoheleth, in his bitterness, doubts whether any human endeavor is worth being pursued, and he comes to the conclusion that Wisdom is beyond man's reach. The most that man is able to do is to live fully the present moment, with its modest joys and pains, its labors and its freedom from cares.

In the Book of Sirach, Wisdom seems less distant. His middle-class common sense makes him search her out in the moderation of desires, in the thankful acceptance of what is given him, in the optimism that all will end by explaining itself, in the admiration of what he understands or does not understand in God's work, in the joy which gives life, and in the calmness of faith which sings the hymn of praise and thanksgiving.

This balance, possible in good times, was broken by a trial as violent as the persecution of the second century.

This search for Wisdom was hesitant and painful. Contradictions seemed to be multiplied. And, yet, each of the great sages conquered a little of the truth: Wisdom is of this world and not of it. She is simultaneously accessible to man, and yet untouchable.

At least, all the teachers of Wisdom agree on one point, each one influenced by his concept of life: they prepared hearts for the personal commitment implied in the setting up of the New Covenant.

Antiochus, in spite of himself, renders invaluable service to Israel's Wisdom by withdrawing her from the narrow limits in which Jewish thought had to embrace her. His persecution tried a fidelity that Wisdom had always preached, and now Israel is on the verge of discovering the limitless perspectives of life which the earth refused to grant it.

The Chosen People's journey, preached with such insistence and continuity by the prophets, ended most surely on the holy Mountain where the eternal kingdom would be established; but

Wisdom, up to this point, had not yet even given a glimpse of how this promise would be concretely realized. In the light of the trial, which should have ruined such a hope, she will lead her children beyond the horizon into a world of the resurrected, into a universe which escapes the constraints and limitations of time. The martyrs will be the seed of the New Israel which will be set up upon the ruins of empires.

The sage, whose mission it was to teach the secret of life, is about to become an apocalyptic writer who will allow the human glance a look at the end of time.

*  *  *

Israel's Wisdom, in opposing the claims of Greek universalism and humanism, had stated her unique character with Sirach's writing. There is the same apologetic pre-occupation in the popular stories of the first chapters of the Book of Daniel: like the story of Joseph at the Pharaoh's court, they bring out the fact that Jewish Wisdom is without equal.

Nebuchadnezzar marvels at finding the young Jews ". . . ten times better than all the magicians and enchanters that were in all the kingdom" (1, 20).

Their immediate and incredible good fortune has no other explanation. Their wisdom alone is capable of answering what the king expects from his wisest men. It is question of mysteries which human prudence is powerless to understand, even at the price of the most alluring promises: "Whoever reads this writing, and shows me its interpretation, shall be clothed with purple, and have a chain of gold around his neck, and shall be the third ruler in the kingdom" (5, 7); and even under the worst threats: ". . . if you do not make known to me the dream and its interpretation, you shall be torn limb from limb, and your houses shall be laid in ruins" (2, 5).

The Chaldean sages, challenged to the impossible, can only stutter: "There is not a man on earth who can meet the king's demand; for no great and powerful king has asked such a thing of any magician or enchanter or Chaldean. The thing that the king asks is difficult, and none can show it to the king except the gods, whose dwelling is not with flesh" (2, 10-11).

When the king commands them to tell him his dream before interpreting it, does he not seem to be forcing them to confess that they have only the light of their own minds and no other lights?

And if Daniel succeeds where they failed, it is not because nature has endowed him with an exceptional penetration of mind. Never of himself would he have been capable of solving the puzzle: "Then Daniel went to his house and made the matter known to Hananiah, Mishael, and Azariah, his companions, and told them to seek mercy of the God of heaven concerning this mystery, so that Daniel and his companions might not perish with the rest of the wise men of Babylon" (2, 17-18).

It is from God that his knowledge will come. "Then the mystery was revealed to Daniel in a vision of the night" (2, 19).

He admits this with fervent humility in a hymn of thanksgiving: "Blessed be the name of God for ever and ever, to whom belong wisdom and might. He reveals deep and mysterious things; he knows what is in the darkness, and the light dwells with him. To thee, O God of my fathers, I give thanks and praise, for thou hast given me wisdom and strength" (2, 20, 22-23).

Nebuchadnezzar acknowledges the supernatural character of this Wisdom; and the queen remembers, when Belshazzar, filled with fear, rivets his eyes on the mysterious writing which his official sages cannot read: "There is a man in your kingdom in whom is the spirit of the holy gods. In the days of your father light and understanding and wisdom, like the wisdom of the gods, were found in him . . ." (5, 11).

God's Wisdom is alone able to penetrate the mystery, since God is master of mystery; it alone can uncover the future, since God is the master of the future.

* * *

Ancient civilizations always had recourse to the knowledge of priests and to the counsel of the wise men before engaging on any enterprise of importance. It was important that the prediction be favorable.

This future, however, was too close to be always impenetrable. The priests at Delphi, consulted by cities and princes, were disposing of a great amount of information. As a consequence they could not fail at times, thanks to their experience and sagacity, to give a probable interpretation to the Pithia's inarticulate cries. Herodotus, who examined the archives of the sanctuary, assured himself of this fact. When the priests were baffled, they saved face by double meaning or by vague predictions.

But, in this case, the future, whose gravity the kings have a confused presentiment and which they are so impatient to examine, is not limited to the immediate present. Beyond these continued tomorrows there is nothing but darkness; and this darkness, no ray pierces, except the ray of one of God's revelations. Thus Daniel can boldly state before Nebuchadnezzar: "No wise men, enchanters, magicians, or astrologers can show to the king the mystery which the king has asked, but there is a God in heaven who reveals mysteries, and he has made known to the King Nebuchadnezzar what will be in the latter days" (2, 27-28).

Because of her divine origin, Jewish Wisdom is not only able to perceive what cannot be grasped by human perspicacity, but she alone enjoys the privilege of knowing that world is directed towards a precise goal and that history is carrying out the plan of the Most High while it is unfolding.

The Greeks, to tell the truth, were too shrewd not to be aware that civilizations are born and die, that the destiny of men is incorporated and explained in their overlapping. The concordance of the dynasty chronicles of the nations furnished the Greeks with a framework sufficient to elaborate a general outline of the history of humanity. Hence that rough survey which has inspired the schema of the "four kingdoms" of the Book of Daniel. Further, these composite states, which Alexander's lieutenants had cut up, did not allow the formation of a national consciousness.

But from all this complexity it was not possible to infer anything else but a certain development of man. The future remained unintelligible to the Greeks: they knew neither the beginning nor the end as far as the movement of the world was concerned.

This lack of certitude seems to be reflected somewhat in the work of Qoheleth; but if Wisdom appears to him as a stranger to earth and as shut up within her own impenetrable secret, he did not doubt her existence. When man failed, God knew the goal towards which humanity was on the march.

Now, however, the mystery, hidden from the eyes of the ancient sages, is revealed. Wisdom gives a glimpse of its distances, the direction of which is clearly delineated and specified. She now knows where the journey is leading. The centuries are only the banks between which the human empires flow and the small states which they drag along after them. Beyond there is the infinity of God's Kingdom:

"And in the days of those kings the God of heaven will set up a kingdom which shall never be destroyed, nor shall its sovereignty be left to another people. It shall break in pieces all these kingdoms and bring them to an end, and it shall stand forever" (2, 44). "And to him was given dominion and glory and kingdom . . . his dominion is an everlasting dominion, which shall not pass away" (7, 14).

While the apocalyptic visions take as their leitmotif the "end of time" and the "last days," each account ends on a note of triumph, honoring the eternal reign of God: "I make a decree that in all my royal dominion men tremble and fear before the God of Daniel, for he is the living God enduring for ever; and his dominion shall be to the end" (6, 27; cf. 3, 45; 4, 31).

This revelation which Israel's Wisdom gives the world is a teaching; it is not simply satisfying vain curiosity. When learning the conclusion of their history, men can orientate themselves to the everlasting kingdom after receiving an exact evaluation of earthly values. The work of Wisdom is crowned in this revelation. The Apocalypse, bringing it to completion, will finally reveal the bright goal of the destiny of those who will not withdraw from God's sustaining hand.

*    *    *

Daniel, no more than the apocalyptic writers, is not a prophet. He has been called one. In contrast to the mission of the sage, the prophet does not confine himself to revealing the route. He walks on the road first in order to bring Israel after him.

Since the persecution of Epiphanes, the sages will not be the last to pay with their lives. They also will be glorified in the judgment, they will give the example of sacrifice: "And those among the people who are wise shall make many understand, though they shall fall by the sword and flame, by captivity and plunder, for some days" (11, 33).

It is less by giving up their life than by their example that they will influence others; it is not they to whom one turns, but rather their teaching. Each one is alone with his responsibilities: "... but the wicked shall do wickedly and none of the wicked shall understand; but those who are wise shall understand" (12, 10).

The visionary presented by the inspired author has certain traits of resemblance to some prophets, especially Ezekiel. At the sound of the divine voice, for instance, Daniel swoons:

"Then I heard the sound of his words, and when I heard the sound of his words, I fell on my face in a deep sleep with my face to the ground. And behold, a hand touched me and set me trembling on hands and knees. And he said to me, 'O Daniel, man greatly beloved, give heed to the words I speak to you, and stand upright, for now I have been sent to you'" (10, 9-11).

This is only a material detail. The personage of Daniel remains without spiritual compactness. In the second part of the Book there is no interlocutor, no combat to sustain. Daniel is not an actor, but a spectator. He is the only one admitted to the contemplation of these visions, he "the man of desires," and he keeps their secret to himself. "As for me, Daniel, my thoughts greatly alarmed me, and my color changed; but I kept the matter in my mind" (7, 28).

The secret will be published much later and it will be unknown generations that will benefit from them: "But you, Daniel, shut up the words, and seal the book, until the time of the end" (12, 4).

As deep as is Daniel's trouble, the course of his life will in no way be modified: "And I, Daniel, was overcome and lay sick for some days; then I rose and went about the king's business; and I was appalled by the vision and did not understand it" (8, 27).

Also, it is not to his courage but his wisdom that the angel Gabriel makes an appeal: "O Daniel, I have come out to give you wisdom and understanding ... therefore consider the word and understand the vision" (9, 22-23).

The end of history cannot be the revelation of a prophet whose action is deeply influenced by his time. Here there is no need to exercise a direct influence on the events. It was the role of the visionary to perceive "beyond time," the dawn of the eternal day.

Just as the sages took at times as their spokesman a man whose legendary prudence made him famous, such as Solomon, whose traditional teaching they took up, extending or enriching it, so the apocalyptic writers attributed their message to some famous ancestor, such as Henoch, Noah, Moses, or one of Jacob's sons. The inspired author makes choice of one of the personages of the Exile to help the Jews understand why the New Covenant, longed for since Jeremiah, was late in being fulfilled.

It is to this sage among sages that he returns to conclude the teaching of his predecessors, opening out a perspective of a resurrection which would no longer be that of a People, but the resurrection of anyone who would remain faithful even to the death.

His teaching, nevertheless, calls for a follow-up. History will not terminate simply because this fact has been unveiled through Wisdom. The advent of the New Covenant, in order that it may become an event, will necessitate the appearance of a Prophet, the last of the prophets who was to be expected, especially from the time of the Maccabees: "And the Jews and their priests decided that Simon should be their leader and high priest for ever, until a trustworthy prophet should arise" (1 Mac. 14, 41).

Knowledge, powerless in itself to set up the Kingdom of God, is confined to preparing for it. It must be exchanged for that manifestation of God's power which St. Paul speaks about: "And I was with you in weakness and in much fear and trembling; and my speech and my message were not in plausible words of wisdom, but in demonstration of the spirit and power, that your faith might not rest in the wisdom of men but in the power of God" (1 Cor. 2, 3-5).

The New Israel will enter into the heavenly sanctuary only through the blood of the high priest: "But when Christ appeared as a high priest of the good things that have come, then through the greater and more perfect tent (not made with hands, that is, not of this creation), he entered once for all into the Holy Place, taking not the blood of goats and calves but his own blood, thus securing an eternal redemption. Therefore he is the mediator of a New Covenant, so that those who are called may receive the promised eternal inheritance, since a death once occurred which redeems them from the transgressions under the first covenant" (Heb. 9, 11-15).

But while waiting for the blood of the Lamb to be shed, the visions of Daniel will remain a closed and sealed book: "Who is worthy to open the scroll and break its seals? . . . Worthy art thou to take the scroll and open its seals, for thou wast slain and by thy blood didst ransom men for God from every tribe and tongue and people and nation, and hast made them a kingdom and priests to our God, and they shall reign on earth" (Apoc. 5, 2, 9-10).

# THE BOOK OF WISDOM

6 We prefer to give this title to this work in order to avoid all confusion between the work itself and its subject.

In the first century before our era, Alexandria was a great city. the Jewish population alone was in the hundreds of thousands. Among these Jews there were those who, because they were highly educated, desired to become involved in Greek society. They desired this not to become hellenized themselves, for they were deeply attached to their faith and traditions, but in order to fight against the many prejúdiced ideas the Greeks had about them. They wanted to make known both the grandeur of their religion and the richness of their wisdom. As it frequently happens, pleading turned to indictment, discussion to preaching. But this did not displease the Greeks who always greatly enjoyed an exchange of ideas.

The author of the Book of Wisdom belonged, without any doubt, to this intellectual Jewish elite. Following the usual literary tradition of his time, he chose Solomon as his mouthpiece, who is addressing kings; in reality, what he intends to do is to capture the attention of the educated public in the capital of the Ptolemies.

We are hesitant about the exact date of the composition of this work; however, we would not be far from wrong in placing it in the first half of the first century before Jesus Christ.

A.- THE JUST ONE DESPISED BY THE WORLD

The Book of Daniel had given a glimpse of a glorious future to the very much mistreated Jews of the second century. This future would be the coming of the New Israel and the Kingdom of God. There would be victory after the sacrilegious attack upon all they held as sacred both in the Temple and in their hearts, and after the death so many of them would undergo in order to remain faithful to these things.

And what a victory this was to be! Having fully become God's people (Ez. 11, 20), not only were they to behold the humbled nations (Jer. 16, 19; Is. 54, 4) coming to Jerusalem, henceforth like "an immovable tent, whose stakes will never be plucked up" (Is. 33, 20), but their own life, apparently uselessly poured out, was going to continue into eternity. For them the words of Isaiah took on their real meaning: "He will swallow up death for ever" (Is. 25, 8).

This victory seemed imminent. However, the Wisdom of God knows no precipitation and the history he directs evolves slowly. It requires time in which to develop. There was much for the Jews to learn before that great day of the Lord, that day towards which they had been on the march for many years and had passed through so many tribulations. Every time they feel they have reached it, only turns out to be another dawn, advancing before them and shedding light upon the rough road ahead, as the Cloud in the Desert.

The persecution of Antiochus preceded the new era just as the triumph of Jerusalem had followed upon Sennacherib's invasion. The trial had ended modestly by the military and political success of the Maccabees and the setting up of an autonomous State.

The outcome was not negligible: the Jews, henceforth sheltered from the attempts of others to assimilate them, maintained inviolate their *religious independence*. But the violence of princes was to be succeeded by something less brutal but just as irritating, viz., the incomprehension and injustice of an attitude to which Israel has never remained indifferent.

This was indeed a new trial for these Jews who, because they realized themselves to be the chosen ones of God, undoubtedly expected others to envy them or at least respect them. This was a trial they had to undergo, but it was a trial from which they would be enriched. Just as the Book of Daniel has aided them in withstanding and overcoming the worst of tyrannies, the Book of Wisdom will teach them how to conduct themselves before the judgment of the world until the time when it will influence this same world.

This trial will be experienced by them after the victory of the Maccabees once their autonomy has been accepted, and this will naturally be outside the limits of Palestine in the colonies of the Diaspora where they will live among strange cultures. As providential as it was, the Hasmonean state could not claim to be the New Israel, for many of its children dispersed throughout the world were subject to powers that had welcomed them. It is, then, the Jews of the Diaspora who will have to take upon themselves the weight of the trial, thus continuing the difficult experience of the Election among the pagans.

The Jews of Palestine will be acquainted only with the profuse literature of the sects which will soon develop there; but it will be at Alexandria that the charism of inspiration will emerge, since it is there that the Jews will have to lay claim to their privilege of being the children of God, in the presence of the hatred of the Copts and the mockery of the Greeks.

       ✿   ✿   ✿

This hostile attitude — we would have called it *antisemitism,* if this word were not both anachronistic and too general — is easily understood if we remember the attitude Israel was taking in the pagan society in which it found itself.

Through its obedience to a Law without analogue, through the strangeness of its customs, through the intransigence of its whole conduct, it made up a *closed and incomprehensible world* in the community in which it was living: "His manner of life is unlike that of others, and his ways are strange" (2, 15).

He dislikes mixing with others as though he ran the risk of soiling himself through contact with them: ". . . he avoids our ways as unclean" (2, 16).

If only he went his way in silence! But he has to censor others boldly: ". . . he opposes our actions; he reproaches us for sins against the law" (2, 12).

Even when he is silent his very presence is a mute condemnation of all the Gentiles: "He became to us the reproof of our thoughts; the very sight of him is a burden to us" (2, 14).

While life is very simple and while the only thing we can do is gather its joys in before it passes off like a shadow (2, 5), the Jew comes to change its whole course. All wish only to live in peace, but he goes about the city like a trouble-maker and an enemy of the human race.

The Jew pushes his pride too far. The Greek world had its haughty and brutal censors; but in this world where philosophers and sages abound, Israel alone pretends to possess the whole truth; it alone thinks itself religious, and worse still, it believes itself an incomparable race and boasts of having special privileges and being the offspring of God: "He professes to have knowledge of God, and calls himself the child of the Lord, and boasts that God is his father" (2, 13, 16).

Who are these Jews who impudently try to teach the older civilizations? The poor relations of a brilliant world, they are nothing but cowardly barbarians and are hardly a nation. The pagans say of them: "What is weak proves itself to be useless" (2, 11).

The contrast is too great between their mediocrity and their presumption for the Greek not to take offense. Since they force themselves under the eyes of others, their misery will be laid

THE BOOK OF WISDOM

bare; and everything then will appear odious: their morality which stifles liberty, their strange cult which despise the gods universally accepted and which is perhaps only a subtle form of atheism, and even their mutual charity is suspect because of its narrowness.

Man does not love what he cannot understand. And the less he understands the more he becomes intolerant.

He will be totally *sceptical*, first of all, of everything that does not enter within the norms of his own thought; he is impatient to see experience confound the heterodox: "Let us see if his words are true, and let us test what will happen at the end of his life; for if the righteous man is God's son, he will help him, and will deliver him from the hand of his adversaries" (2, 17-18).

He is irritated by every form of superiority, pretended or real. To him great virtues is nothing but affection, firm faith, nothing but presumption. In his irritation he is tempted not even to wait until experience removes the mask: "Let us test him with insult and torture, that we may find out how gentle he is, and make trial of his forbearance. Let us condemn him to a shameful death, for, according to what he says, he will be protected" (2, 19-20).

Will we hear this *shameful mockery* at the foot of the Cross? (Matt. 27, 39-43).

But hatred still remains a form of esteem. Is the Jew worth the movement of anger? It is enough to treat him with contempt instead of making fun of him or spitting at him: "They will see him, and have contempt for him" (4, 18).

Does the Jew observe this *contempt?* As frequently happens this is found upon hasty judgments which quickly degenerate into calumnies. It is so easy to enlarge on what one does not know.

The Jews know this already, and the abject accusations which are spread about them, they will one day share with the Christians throughout the Roman empire.

But what was this humiliating set-back of the Jews when they confronted the hatred which weighed down upon their poor

community with the promise of the universal kingdom of God
which was to be theirs!

❋    ❋    ❋

In the presence of this universal hatred, there must have been
no lack of pusillanimous Jews who tried their best to escape its
ravages. Perhaps they used Ben Sirach's advice as an excuse for
not frequenting the company of the wicked: "Refrain from strife
and you will lessen sins" (Eccl. 28, 8).

Perhaps, too, being very honest with themselves, they admitted that not every man could "go about the city battlements"
with intrepidity (Eccl. 9, 13).

The times were no longer, however, for the prudent or the
timid. After all, if "another keeps silent because he knows when
to speak" (Eccl. 20, 6), the hour has come to speak. And it will
always be Wisdom's honor for having supported those who defied
this hour.

Far from fleeing from reproaches, she will take them one
by one in order to turn them into titles of glory.

If the pagans turn her into ridicule, it is because their human
weakness does not allow them to raise themselves above the appearances of a corrupt world to look on eternal realities: "Their
wickedness blinded them, and they did not know the secret pur-
poses of God, nor hope for the wages of holiness, nor discern the
prize of blameless souls; for God created man for incorruption,
and made him in the image of his own eternity" (2, 21-23).

Their vision is too short-sighted to discern the evident protection that God extends to his Elect: "Yet the peoples saw and
did not understand, nor take such a thing to heart, that God's
grace and mercy are with his Elect" (4, 15).

But negation does not prevent what is to go on existing. One
depreciated Israel's morality in vain, for it still had as its legislator the God who will judge all men: "For inquiry will be
made into the counsels of an ungodly man, and a report of his

words will come to the Lord, to convict him of his lawless deeds; because a jealous ear hears all things" (1, 9-10).

Let the scoffers berate the Jews for impudence and folly, they will still have to confess as did the enemies of Israel in this same Egypt over the bodies of their first-born: "this people is the son of God" (18, 13), and that they have been chosen by him who has placed his sovereign hand over them: "and the faithful will abide with him in love, because grace and mercy are upon his elect" (3, 9; cf. 4, 15). No human power will deprive of his protection: "But the souls of the righteous are in the hand of God, and no torment will ever touch them" (3, 1). Never will his care for them cease: "... the Most Hight takes care of them" (5, 15).

This Credo is not new, but what is new is that Wisdom proclaims it to the world.

❋   ❋   ❋

On this last point there are undoubtedly some Greeks who would accuse Jewish Wisdom of having plagiarized the idea of Providence from the Stoics.

True, the inspired author wishing to make himself understood by the pagans has not hesitated at times to speak their own language. Nonetheless he evokes Yahweh, the traditional God of armies, the Lord of creation, who, in the noise of the storm, raises up all the forces of nature to defend his People when he judges it opportune: "The Lord will take his zeal as his whole armor; and will arm all creation to repel his enemies; he will put on righteousness as a breastplate, and wear impartial justice as a helmet; he will take holiness as an invincible shield, and sharpen stern wrath for a sword, and creation will join with him to fight against the madmen. Shafts of lightning will fly with true aim, and will leap to the target as from a well-drawn bow of clouds, and hailstones full of wrath will be hurled as from a catapult; the water of the sea will rage against them, and rivers will relentlessly overwhelm them; a mighty wind will rise against them, and like a tempest it will winnow them away" (5, 17-23).

How confound this personal interest that God has in his children with the providential government of the world, such as the Stoics conceive? The Most High is ready to turn laws of creation upside down in a miraculous manner in favor of his own. The elements change their properties at a word from him: "For, most incredible of all, in the water, which quenches all things, the fire has still greater effect, for the universe defends the righteous. . . . Snow and ice withstood fire without melting" (15, 17, 22). "Flames, on the contrary, failed to consume the flesh of perishable creatures that walked among them" (19, 21).

And it did not even melt the manna, "the easily melted kind of heavenly food" (19, 21).

Though the inspired author seems to accept without any difficulty the Greek idea of a cosmic order with strict laws, he admits, on the whole, that the one who made these laws can also modify them when he judges it proper: "For the whole creation in its nature was fashioned anew, complying with thy commands, that thy children might be kept unharmed" (19, 6).

The rigidity of nature is not such that the Father's will does not relax in spite of his love: "For the creation, serving thee who has made it, exerts itself to punish the unrighteous, and in kindness relaxes on behalf of those who trust in thee" (16, 24).

We are far from Greek thought here. Whatever lofty idea it could have formed of man's supremacy over the universe, or better, of mind over matter, never would it have admitted that the orderly cosmos could have been placed at the service of individuals, even though they were privileged and superior.

✿   ✿   ✿

Whether God suspends nature's laws or not, he does attach himself to his Elect and protects them with jealous care. Through his prodigies or chastisements, through his Law or his Wisdom, he is near them everywhere and at all times. The Apostle will some day sum up this great biblical concept: "We know that in everything God works for the good with those who love him, who are called according to his purpose" (Rom. 8, 28).

It is because they belong to God, and no power in the world has in itself the least right over them. The authority of princes is exercised in their regard only insofar as he has delegated this authority over them. If God has not chosen them as lieutenants, it is not the Jews who come under the jurisdiction of their tribunal, but the kings who come under that of God. And they dare to cry out before the great ones of the earth: "Listen, therefore, O kings, and understand; learn, O judges of the ends of the earth. Give ear, you that rule over multitudes, and boast of many nations. For your dominion was given you from the Lord, and your sovereignty from the Most High, who will search out your works and inquire into your plans" (6, 1-3).

There is only one Justice and God's evil lieutenants, those who transgress his will, will experience its vigor: "Because as servants of his kingdom you did not rule rightly, nor keep the law, nor walk according to the purpose of God, he will come upon you terribly and swiftly, because severe judgment falls on those in high places" (6, 4-5).

In this Justice there is place for clemency and this will go first to the humble: "For the lowliest man may be pardoned in mercy" (6, 6).

This does not mean that God's saints will be protected from trials and reverses. They can, through weakness, stray from the flock, but the divine shepherd knows they are not there and goes out in search of them. Holiness is not an easy road and its reward is not acquired without suffering: "Having been disciplined a little, they will receive great good, because God tested them and found them worthy of himself; like gold in the furnace he tried them . . ." (3, 5-6). "She gave to holy men the reward of their labors" (10, 17).

The chastisement of the Elect has nothing in common with

that of the wicked. The one is medicinal: "For though in the sight of men they were punished, their hope is full of immortality. Having been disciplined a little, they will receive great good" (3, 4-5). The punishment of the wicked is afflictive: "For thou didst test them as a father does in warning, but thou didst examine the ungodly as a stern judge does in condemnation" (11, 10; cf. 12, 22).

If one punishment is temporary, the other is definitive. The author of Wisdom illustrates it by the traditional memories of Israel's history.

For instance, in the desert the thirsty Hebrews after three days march despair of being able to drink the waters of Marah. At the intercession of Moses Yahweh makes the waters sweet and they quenched their thirst before camping near the twelve springs of Elim; again, at Raphidim, Yahweh made water spring from the rock, while the Egyptians thirsted near the waters of the Nile, "stirred up and defiled with blood" (11, 6). "For when they tried, though they were being disciplined in mercy, they learned how the ungodly were tormented when judged in wrath" (11, 9).

Again, in the desert of Sin, Yahweh, with manna, rained down quail with which Israel satisfied its hunger "after suffering a short time" (16, 3), while Pharaoh's subjects, "when they desired food, might lose the least remnant of appetite because of the odious creatures sent to them" (16, 3).

At the time when the Egyptians, molested by grasshoppers and flies, perished without any possible remedy, the Hebrews, threatened by more fearsome beasts, were saved not by the sign of salvation which reminded them of the Law, but by the "Savior of all" (16, 6-7). "Thy wrath did not continue to the end; they were troubled for a little while as a warning" (16, 5-6).

God does not deal with friends and enemies alike. Through these examples he wants to make it understood that, though man can suffer death and even inflict it, he is still not master of life; "He cannot bring back the departed spirit" (16, 14).

God alone enjoys this power: "For thou hast power over life and death; thou dost lead to the gates of hades and back again" (16, 13).

And it is really of this that Jewish Wisdom seeks to convince her detractors. The Greeks, in fact, ironically objected that Israel's lot was not preferable to their own: did not death overtake each in turn? But for the Jew death does not end everything: "The righteous live forever, and their reward is with the Lord" (5, 15).

Death is the threshhold leading to a mysterious peace: "For they will see the end of the wise man, and will not understand what the Lord proposed for him, and for what he kept him safe" (4, 17).

Even an early death is still a grace for him: "But the righteous man, though he die early, will be at rest" (4, 7). "For the soul was pleasing to the Lord, therefore he took him quickly from the midst of wickness" (4, 14).

✿   ✿   ✿

Greek philosophy was able to claim that Israel's teaching on the *immortality of the soul* was plagiarized from it.

Jewish Wisdom, assimilating the notion, had singularly enriched its content. When she revealed the privileged lot reserved for the just, after death as well as during life, she made its concept very explicit, which was something the philosophers never had succeeded in doing.

Moreover, the certitude which this notion of immortality brought him, and which Wisdom had so strongly made her own, only imperfectly consoled the Jew for the contempt heaped upon him. His intuition enriched it with the traditional theme of the revenge which, at the coming of the kingdom of God, the just will take on the world: "In the time of their visitation they will shine forth, and will run like sparks through the stubble. They will govern nations and rule over peoples, and the Lord will reign over them forever" (3, 7-8).

*Revenge without bitterness*: for Israel there was no question of rejoicing over the abasement of the gentiles, but of being God's witness and the guide of nations, instructing them through its triumph. There will no longer be any need for contempt when the world, recognizing the grandeur of the Jews, will now understand the promises that Israel had received.

Their eyes will be opened like the eyes of the Egyptians of old who, from the darkness into which they were plunged, they heard the Hebrews singing "in full light." "And they were thankful that thy holy ones, though previously wronged, were doing them no injury" (18, 1).

In their miseries these enemies of Israel: "... were equally distressed, for a twofold grief possessed them, and a groaning at the memory of what had occurred. For when they heard that through their own punishments the righteous had received benefit, they perceived it was the Lord's doing. For though they had mockingly rejected him who long before had been cast out and exposed, at the end of the events they marveled at him, for their thirst was not like that of the righteous" (11, 12-14).

What was true yesterday will be true tomorrow. The day will come when the Jew, rehabilitated in the eyes of the world, will inspire remorse in all, heralding conversion: "Then the righteous man will stand with great confidence in the presence of those who have afflicted him, and those who made light of his labors. When they see him, they will be shaken with dreadful fear, and they will speak to one another in repentance, and in anguish of spirit they will groan, and say, 'This is the man who we once held in derision and made a byword of reproach, we fools! We thought that his life was madness and that his end was without honor. Why has he been numbered among the sons of God?'" (5, 1-5).

Eternal values cannot be compared with human values. The "son of God" is poor, weak, and humiliated. Far from taking anything away from his grandeur, this apparent disgrace adds to it and we shall see later that it is a *conditio sine qua non*.

The contempt he bears prefigures the Cross which the Just One *par excellence* will carry. His haggard and troubled features hide from the insulting crowd the marvelous secret of his Election, just as the face of the most misunderstood of the persecuted will hide his divine origin from those striking him.

Since the Exile the mystery of poverty has puzzled the Jews. Israel's Wisdom was unable to penetrate its mystery immediately, but she revealed its spiritual meaning little by little to the admiration of all. Poverty appeared to her as the attitude of humility, self-surrender, the dependability and expectation of him who has nothing from him who has all; poverty is the means of most surely being clothed with imperishable riches.

Wisdom will succeed in freeing Israel from the idolatrous worship of power and force, riches and pride. Not knowing how to rid itself of these will be Islam's misfortune.

In a little unknown town in Judea, soon an unknown virgin, poor in this world's possessions, but much poorer in herself, will sing that God satisfied the hungry and the famished while he sends the rich empty away. It is because she possessed nothing of herself that she will receive all and generations will call her blessed.

### B.- THE PRIVILEGE OF WISDOM

Alexandria, the capital of Hellenism, shone forth with all the splendor of her philosophy, art, and science. She had gathered together the heritage of poets, historians, orators, and philosophers, who had made of Greece the most cultured people in the world. This people had been refined by centuries of dialectics and familiarity with a sense of beauty and grace that attracted the eyes and ears and minds of all. Sophocles and Aristophanes had so perfected their art that they were listened too equally by the educated and the uneducated; Herodotus had drawn the crowds from the Olympic games to the reading of his books, just as the bards of the Homeric songs enchanted their listeners. Socrates and Demosthenes succeeded in making the ordinary people reflect and meditate.

And it was to this great and difficult people that the despised Jew dares to speak of his superiority!

In his feverish attempts at emulation he entered the fields of entertainment, philosophy, and history. And more boldly still, he claimed in the presence of anyone willing to listen that the world had never produced anything of the great and the beautiful which it did not receive from Israel. Did not the Greek philosophers plagiarize from Moses? And did not the Jewish Sibyl accuse Homer of stealing her secrets?

With the exception of Philo, however, no personality emerged from Judaism who merited the attention of Alexandria's educated classes.

The pretentions of the Jew carried him away. Israel's true grandeur is to be found neither in profane literature, nor in the sciences, nor in art, but solely in Wisdom freely given to him by God. To possess her was to possess all things. The rest, from which Greece drew such pride, was nothing in comparison with her. And the Jews in their passionate desire to confront the greatest pagan civilizations had evidently forgotten this, "Ah, if you had known the gift of God . . ." (Jn. 4, 10).

❊   ❊   ❊

The Wisdom of Israel's incomparable glory is to give to existence both its deep meaning and its real worth.

The Greeks, clever, at handling ideas, had undoubtedly built up an admirable philosophical system, but the essential was missing because they were unaware of where life is going and what its true purpose is.

Although the author of Wisdom somewhat jars the thinking

of a large educated class, he vigorously outlines the *fundamental despair of the pagan*:

"Short and sorrowful is our life, and there is no remedy when a man comes to his end, and no one has been known to return from Hades. Because we were born by mere chance, and hereafter we shall be as though we had never been; because the breath of our nostrils is smoke, and reason is a spark kindled by the beating of our hearts. When it is extinguished, the body will turn to ashes, and the spirit will dissolve in empty air. Our name will be forgotten in time, and no one will remember our works; our life will pass away like the traces of a cloud, and be scattered like mist that is chased by the rays of the sun and overcome by its heat. For our allotted time is the passing of a shadow, and there is no return from our death, because it is sealed up and no one turns back" (2, 1-5).

With such a point of departure the inspired author logically elucidates the Greek way of life, which will find all too many followers in imperial Rome: "Come, therefore, let us enjoy the good things that exist, and make use of the creation to the full as in youth. Let us take our fill of costly wine and perfumes, and let no flower of spring pass by us. Let us crown ourselves with rosebuds before they wither. Let none of us fail to share in our revelry, everywhere let us leave signs of enjoyment, because this is our portion, and this our lot" (2, 6-9).

This is like a page from Horace. We may remind ourselves here of how much the pagan's *"carpe diem"* differs from that of Qoheleth's. Between the two there is nothing in common except a straightforward look at life in this world and the fleetingness of time. When denouncing the vanity of Israel's earthly dreams, Qoheleth had no thought of denying the value of existence. Would he ever have written that man is the child of chance? Would he, to console himself for his troubles and to become interested in this passing life, deliver himself up to his base instincts? In spite of his apparent pessimism, real or affected, Qoheleth knows the great secret that transfigures our human existence: "The end of the matter; all has been heard. Fear God, keep the commandments; for this is the whole duty of man. For God will bring every deed into judgment, with every secret thing, whether good or evil" (Eccl. 12, 13-14).

Developing his strong satire the author of Wisdom oversteps common truth in his generalizations; however, he is trying to open the wound to lay bare the real consequences which are always present in germ, viz., man, without a set of morals, seeks only self-satisfaction and knows no obstacle, and his avidity will soon precipitate him into crime and injustice: "Let us oppress the righteous poor man; let us not spare the widow nor regard the gray hairs of the aged. . . . Let us lie in wait for the righteous man, because he is inconvenient to us and opposes our actions" (2, 10-12).

How empty and unbalanced is the life of the impious! "Wisdom has built her house, and has set up seven pillars" (Prov. 9, 1); "Wisdom gives strength to the wise man more than ten rulers who are in a city" (Eccles. 7, 19); ". . . the man who leans on her will not fall" (Eccl. 15, 4). On the contrary, the impious man is powerless to establish a family worthy of himself: "Their wives are foolish, and their children evil" (3, 12); his activity has no meaning: "Their hope is vain, their labors are unprofitable, and their works are useless" (3, 11).

What good is old age to him? "Even if they live long they will be held of no account, and finally their old age will be without honor" (3, 17).

The children he leaves behind, being like him, will only prolong his uselessness: "But the prolific brood of the ungodly will be of no use, and none of their illegitimate seedlings will strike a deep root or take a firm hold. . . . For children born of unlawful unions are witnesses of evil against their parents when God examines them" (4, 3, 6).

He passes over the earth, not like one alive, but like a phantom who "is dispersed like smoke before the wind" (5, 14). "What has arrogance profited us? And what has our boasted wealth brought us? All these things have vanished like a shadow, and like a rumor that passes by; like a ship that sails through the billowy water, and when it has passed no trace can be found, nor track of its keel in the waves; or as, when a bird flies through the air, no evidence of its passage is found; the light air, lashed by the beat of its pinions and pierced by the force of its rushing flight, is traversed by the movement of its wings, and afterward no sign of its coming is found there. . . . So we also, as soon as we were born, ceased to be, and we had no sign of virtue to show, but were consumed in our wickedness" (5, 8-13).

Israel talks from its own experience. It honestly admits its past errors which blurred its path: "So it was we who strayed from the way of truth, and the light of righteousness did not shine on us, and the sun did not rise upon us. We took our fill of the paths of lawlessness and destruction, and we journeyed through trackless deserts, but the way of the Lord we have not known" (5, 6-7).

Israel, however, placed itself once more under God's hand, while the impious, refusing to know the living God, delivers himself hand and foot to the most insidious idolatries. Thus he throws himself gradually into the worst of crimes: "For whether they kill children in their initiations, or celebrate secret mysteries, or hold frenzied revels with strange customs, they no longer keep either their lives or their marriages pure, but they either treacherously kill one another, or grieve one another by adultery, and all is a raging riot of blood and murder, theft, and deceit, corruption, faithlessness, tumult, perjury, confusion over what is good, forgetfulness of favors, pollution of souls, sex perversion, disorder in marriage, adultery, and debauchery" (14, 23-26).

Worse still, they become hardened in this way and even experience a terrible peace: "Afterward it was not enough for them to err about the knowledge of God, but they live in great strife due to ignorance, and they call such great evils peace" (14, 22).

The Apostle will be no more indulgent with paganism when

he recalls the same griefs. The pagan, when it is question of God, prostituted himself to a falsehood: "Therefore God gave them up in the lust of their hearts to impurity, to the dishonoring of their bodies among themselves, because they exchanged the truth about God for a lie and worshipped and served the creature rather than the Creator, who is blessed for ever and ever. Amen" (Rom. 1, 24-25).

Thick darkness shrouds the pagan world, a darkness similar to that which weighed upon Egypt at the time of the Exodus: "For when lawless men supposed that they held the holy nation in their power, they themselves lay as captives of darkness and prisoners of long night, shut in under their roofs, exiles from eternal providence" (17,2).

✿   ✿   ✿

After painting the portrait of the impious man in such somber colors, Wisdom's author brings out the divine characteristics of Wisdom with a pencil of light.

Everything in Wisdom is light, that beautiful golden light which bathed the Hebrews: "But for thy holy ones there was great light" (18, 1).

The reason for this is that Wisdom and the notion of light are inseparable: " . . . and I chose to have her rather than light, because her radiance never ceases" (7, 10). "For she is more beautiful than the sun, and excels every constellation of the stars. Compared with the light she is found to be superior, for it is succeeded by night, but against wisdom evil does not prevail" (7, 29-30).

In its mysterious journey the Chosen People do not travel at random but without hesitation and hindrance, for it advances along a route that stretches out in full brightness: "She guided him on straight paths . . ." (10, 10).

This route, far from hiding the snares of death, leads to life: "And thus the paths of those on earth were set right" (9, 18).

"... because God did not make death, and he does not delight in the death of the living. For he created all things that they might exist, and the generative forces of the world are wholesome, and there is no destructive poison in them; and the dominion of Hades is not on earth. For righteousness is immortal" (1, 13-15).

The life of the just has the same duration as that from which it proceeds: "But the righteous live for ever" (5, 15). "... their hope is full of immortality" (3, 4).

Death is only apparent, and the peace upon which it opens is not illusory or torpid, like that of the pagans, but compact, unalterable, and living: "In the eyes of the foolish they seemed to have died and their departure was thought to be an affliction, and their going from us to be their destruction; but they are at peace" (3, 2-3).

Once the threshold of time is crossed, Wisdom leads where "virtue marches crowned in triumph, victor in the contest for prizes that are undefiled" (4, 2).

Eternal life, however, is not confined to the great beyond as an unverifiable promise. Although it is outside the bounds of time that it receives its full development, yet it begins here below. Time is not erased by eternity, but eternity impregnates time, it saturates it. Far from limiting human possibilities, eternity enlarges these possibilities to infinitude.

What gives value to life is no longer its duration which the old sages spoke of as being a divine blessing; now the compactness which Wisdom will give to it is its real worth: "For age is not honored for length of time, nor measured by number of years; but understanding is gray hairs for men, and a blameless life is ripe old age" (4, 8-9).

Why should one mourn the untimely death of the just? "Being perfected in a short time, he fulfilled long years" (4, 13).

Since human destiny is longer to be found between the time of one's birth and his death, it is foolish to expect everything here below. Among all the goods offered him by Wisdom, the just man will know how to make the proper choice in order to make his life meaningful.

Solomon, presented to us in the Book of Wisdom, speaks as a king and does not forget military glory. As peaceful as he is, the sacred author is nevertheless sensitive to the prestige of Alexandria: "... dread monarchs will be afraid of me when they hear me; among the people I shall show myself capable, and courageous in war" (8, 15).

Solomon is only a fictitious personage in the book. In the Hellenistic world, offspring of the old democracies, the king appeared as an accomplished man in whom all men were represented. Thus the sage, who makes Solomon speak, will express his real ambition: "And if anyone loves righteousness, her labors are virtues; for she teaches self-control and prudence, justice, and courage; nothing in life is more profitable for men than these. And if anyone longs for wide experience, she knows the things of old, and infers the things to come; she understands turns of speech and the solution of riddles; she has foreknowledge of signs and wonders and of the outcome of seasons and times" (8, 7-8).

Great virtue and vast knowledge appear to him as eminently desirable. Each leads to God. They permit the king to shine in the company of his subjects, like the old man rich in experiences shining in the council of the ancients: "Because of her I shall have glory among the multitudes and honor in the presence of the elders, though I am young. I shall be found keen in judgment, and in the sight of rulers I shall be admired. When I am silent they will wait for me, and when I speak they will give heed; and when I speak at greater length they will put their hands on their mouths. Because of her I shall have immortality, and leave an everlasting remembrance to those who come after me" (8, 10-13).

The most beautiful and legitimate glories awaiting him are not the force of arms and the power of edicts but his spiritual prestige. Wisdom will clothe him with this as with an imperial crown, making him realize his true vocation which is "to rule the world in holiness and righteousness, and pronounce judgment in uprightness of soul" (9, 3).

And this is the message that the Jew cries out to the powerful who surround him and who mock him because of the inferior role to which such a morality seems to condemn him. The Wisdom of Israel, though she promises immortality, is not disincarnate; she is not uninterested in time; she lays claim to the knowledge of the art of governing the universe.

Solomon states this clearly: "I learned both what is secret and what is manifest, for Wisdom, the fashioner of all things, taught me. For in her there is a spirit that is intelligent, holy, unique, manifold, subtle, mobile, clear, unpolluted, distinct, invulnerable, loving the good, keen, irresistible, beneficent, humane, steadfast, sure, free from anxiety, all-powerful, overseeing all, and penetrating through all spirits that are intelligent and pure and most subtle" (7, 21-22; cf. 23-27).

If Wisdom can make her disciple master of the world, it is because, taught by her, he knows what other men do not know: "For what man can learn the counsel of God? Or who can discern what the Lord wills? For the reasoning of mortals is worthless, and our designs are likely to fail, for a perishable body weighs down the soul, and this earthly tent burdens the thoughtful mind. We can hardly guess at what is on the earth, and what is at hand we find with labor; but who has traced out what is in the heavens? Who has learned thy counsel, unless thou hast given wisdom and sent thy holy Spirit from on high?" (9, 13-17).

Qoheleth despaired of finding Wisdom here on earth. She seemed to him to have withdrawn from human horizons and to be lost in impenetrable mystery. Here she makes her return in the Book of Wisdom the bearer of immortality, taking her place in the midst of her children. She sows the seed of infinity in their hearts. She who has "shown the kingdom of God" (10, 10) to Jacob, now introduces the just man into God's mystery: "Though she is but one, she can do all things, and while remaining in herself, she renews all things; in every generation she passes into holy souls and makes them friends of God and prophets; for God loves nothing so much as the man who lives with wisdom" (7, 27-28).

She does not call to him from some heavenly realm, but she visits him in his own world where he lives out his destiny, just as she visited Joseph in his prison. Man has only to desire it: "With thee is Wisdom, who knows thy works and was present when thou didst make the world, and who understands what is pleasing in thy sight and what is right according to thy commandments. Send her forth from the holy heavens, and from the throne of thy glory send her, that she may be with me and toil, and that I may learn what is pleasing to thee" (9, 9-10).

*  *  *

This parallel with such violent contrasts was the proudest and noblest response that the "barbarous" Jew could make to the sarcastic remarks of the Greeks. The Greeks, ignorant of life's meaning, were incapable of making it fruitful; the Jew, because he has learned life's meaning from Wisdom, sees this life filled with the divinity which germinates and grows here before coming to full maturity in eternity.

But how does one acquire such a Wisdom, who allows the Jew to teach the Greeks and the whole world? No one can attain her on his own strength. Neither reason nor intuition are sufficient in themselves, for she is a *free gift* of God.

If Solomon receives this gift, it is because he first recognized his native misery. He does not allow himself to be divinized by a credulous people as did other earthly rulers. He knows that, even as king, he has nothing in him more than the ordinary man: "I also am mortal like all men, a descendant of the first-formed child of earth; and in the womb of a mother I was molded into flesh, within the period of ten months, compacted with blood, from the seed of a man and the pleasure of marriage. And when

I was born, I began to breathe the common air, and fell upon the kindred earth, and my first sound was a cry, like that of all. I was nursed with care in swaddling cloths. For no king has had a different beginning of existence; there is for all mankind one entrance into life, and a common departure" (7, 1-6).

To receive Wisdom he made his soul clean, keeping his heart simple and upright: "For perverse thoughts separate men from God, and when his power is tested, it convicts the foolish; because wisdom will not enter a deceitful soul, nor dwell in a body enslaved in sin. For a holy and disciplined spirit will flee from deceit, and will rise and depart from foolish thoughts, and will be ashamed at the approach of unrighteousness" (1, 3-5).

It is not sufficient to be naturally good as was Solomon: "As a child I was by nature well-endowed, and a good soul fell to my lot; or rather, being good, I entered an undefiled body" (8, 19-20).

God's gift is given only to the one who asks for it: "But I perceived that I would not possess wisdom unless God gave her to me, and it was a mark of insight to know whose gift she was, so I appealed to the Lord and besought him . . ." (8, 21).

What is the request, however, if the heart itself is not totally desirous and open to receive Wisdom: "Love righteousness, you rulers of the earth, think of the Lord with uprightness, and seek him with sincerity of heart; because he is found by those who do not put him to the test, and manifests himself to those who do not distrust him" (1, 1-2).

This desire, strong and fervent, must precede the gift, as the lover goes in search of the beloved: "I loved her and sought her from my youth, and I desired to take her for my bride, and I became enamored of her beauty" (8, 2).

One cannot find what he did not seek. Love calls to love: "Wisdom is radiant and unfading, and she is easily discerned by those who love her, and is found by those who seek her. She hastens to make herself known to those who desire her. He who rises early to seek her will have no difficulty, for he will find her sitting at his gates. To fix one's thoughts on her is perfect under-standing, and he who is vigilant on her account will soon be free from care, because she goes about seeking those worthy of her, and she graciously appears to them in their paths, and meets them in every thought. The beginning of wisdom is the most sincere desire for instruction, and concern for instruction is love of her, and love of her is keeping of her laws ..." (6, 12-17).

Wisdom will then establish the kingdom of God in hearts. This life which has no end will commence in each heart.

       ✿    ✿    ✿

The lesson holds for the pagan world that desires nothing beyond what the earth can offer. It holds for Israel also, tempted as it is to place itself on a level with the Greeks whom it ad-mires, though it looks down upon them. Israel's greatness, eclips-ing all other human greatness whether in philosophy or art, is to have been chosen by God to be under his hand and to allow itself to be guided by his Wisdom: ... for even if one is perfect among the sons of men, yet without the wisdom that comes from thee he will be regarded as nothing" (9, 6).

Let the Jew, guided by false excuses, no longer believe that he hastens the advent of God's kingdom by consenting to any new syncretism, which is more dangerous and subtle than the one condemned by the prophets! Failure is better than com-promise; isolation is preferable to agreement bought at the price of unworthy tolerances. Such an agreement, besides being only illusory and transient, without winning the pagan world to the truth, would bring down Israel to the level of "children of an adultery," and "the offspring of an unlawful union will perish" (3, 16). Isolation will perhaps reduce Israel to the state of ap-parent impotency, but it will at least protect the validity of its testimony: "Better than this is childlessness with virtue" (4, 1).

The efficacy of works always escapes human understanding. The Book of Wisdom, surpassing the trial of faith imposed upon so many women of the Bible, from Sarah to Elizabeth, boldly affirms that God can, through the most astounding of contradictions, render the most desperate case of sterility abundantly fertile: "For blessed is the barren woman who is undefiled, who has not entered into a sinful union; she will have fruit when God examines souls" (3, 13).

Had the Virgin of Nazareth meditated upon these words when she consecrated her virginity to the Lord, leaving to him alone the care of rendering her life fruitful? "Sin, O barren one, who did not bear; break forth into singing and cry aloud, you who have not been in travail! For the children of the desolate one will be more than the children of her that is married, says the Lord" (Is. 54, 1).

### C.- THE UNIVERSE IS INVITED TO CONVERSION

In vain did the author of Wisdom make use of his vigorous eloquence, contrasting the empty wisdom of the pagans with the unshakable Wisdom of Israel, the dead works of the one with the saving action of the other, the impure springs from which the impious drank draughts of error, falsehood, and folly with the holy waters which filled the Chosen People with light, strength, and life. The Jews were still forced, if they would escape the contemptuous hostility of the Gentiles, to withdraw to their ghettos in Alexandria.

However, because they realized they were under the hand of God, they were assured of being stronger. The sensible realities that can cruelly wound them, are not able to destroy their faith and their hope. Poor and humiliated, they believe that God is as much among them as if he were holding them up as torches for the universe. They are conscious of retaining infinite and everlasting truth.

If, according to the human way of looking at things, this is not a triumph, if nothing appeared changed in their wretched condition, they have no need for awaiting the revenge promised in their apocalypses in order to taste in advance the joy of victory;

they already experience this secretly in their hearts. When and how that blessed hour of the "shalom" will come, they don't know any more than Job knew how to solve the mystery that encompassed him. But, though the future is hidden, though God guards its secret, they are happier than Job, who was able only to lie prostrate in the dust in the magnificent obscurity of his faith. They look with assurance to the future, and they already discern with joy its coming brightness.

*    *    *

One of the most astonishing characteristics of Israel is its faculty of hoping, which seems to grow stronger the more it is crushed. As long as there was a chance to continue the war in Jerusalem, Jeremiah remained the prophet of doom; but when all was lost, never did he manifest a most exalted faith.

Now the Jews are so sure of victory that will bear witness to the almighty power of God that they dare raise their voices, not only to justify themselves, but to invite the nations to observe their law.

Far from hiding jealously the treasure of Wisdom that knows the mystery of life and has the power to save the whole of humanity, far from concealing, as the initiated do their secrets, the knowledge revealed to them by God, these so-called enemies of the human race are impatient to communicate this knowledge to the whole world: "I will tell you what wisdom is and how she came to be, and I will hide no secrets from you, but I will trace her course from the beginning of creation, and make the knowledge of her clear, and I will not pass by the truth; neither will I travel in the company of sick envy, for envy does not associate with wisdom. A multitude of wise men is the salvation of the world, and a sensible king is the stability of his people. Therefore be instructed by my words, and you will profit" (6, 22-26).

This is how Solomon speaks of kings. He upbraids them, offers them his experience, unveils unheard of riches to them, and calls upon them to follow his example. "Love righteousness, you rulers of the earth, think of the Lord with righteousness" (1, 1).

He urges them fraternally to live according to this Wisdom: "To you then, O Monarchs, my words are directed, that you may learn wisdom and not transgress. For they will be made holy who observe holy things in holiness, and those who have been taught them will find a defense. Therefore set your desire upon my words, long for them, and you will be instructed" (6, 9-11; cf. 6, 1).

It was natural for Wisdom to address first those who "rule over peoples," but this appeal of a king to kings aims at reaching a limitless audience. It is the call of Israel to the whole world.

●   ●   ●

Though the Jews hold themselves aloof from the Gentiles, it is not through aversion or pride, but because of fidelity to these same religious traditions (to this faith, which the Gentiles through ignorance despise, but which will one day be the world's salvation). It is for the good of all that the Jews preserve their heritage.

Wisdom excludes no one when addressing man. "For wisdom is a kindly spirit" (1, 6). "For in her there is a spirit that is beneficent, human..." (7, 23).

Because she loves the human race her disciple cannot look at it otherwise: "Through such work thou hast taught thy people, that the righteous man must be kind..." (12, 19).

Not kind in the sense that the best of pagans understand it, who give their benevolence or their pity to the conquered or their slaves. The kindness of the just man is based on a sentiment of solidarity and on the love that is in Wisdom.

Until the present the prophets and sages were more preoccupied with Israel's evils than with those of the stranger. When Jonas is commanded to preach penance to the Ninivites, he is so astounded at this apparent abnormality that he tries to avoid this unusual mission. The author of Wisdom experiences no repugnance at preaching to all nations, and he does this so willingly that he seems to be preaching to no one else.

*   *   *

He commences by explaining the origin of evil.

The prophets ascribed this origin to bad kings such as Ahaz, Manasseh, and Jehoiakim; the apocalypses ascribed it to the decline of Babylon (Daniel); or at the time of the Deluge (Henoch), it was centered upon the apostasy of the children of the Covenant.

For Wisdom, on the contrary, what creates the problem is the sin that preys upon humanity as a whole. She was also led to go far beyond time in order to find the source of evil. From the very beginning of history the work of God has been corrupted: "God created man for incorruption, and made him in the image of his eternity, but through the devil's envy death entered the world" (2, 23-24).

St. Paul goes back to Adam: "Through one man sin came into the world, and through sin death" (Rom. 5, 12).

If things are such, then the promises of life and the threats of death, which, in the economy of the Covenant, sanctioned Israel's fidelity, are valid for the whole human race. Hence Wisdom is justified in extending to all the exhortation so frequently heard by the Chosen People: "Do not invite death by the error of your life, nor bring on destruction by the works of your hands" (1, 12). She is justified too in giving them the assurance of divine love, the bearer of strength and life: "God did not make death, and he does not delight in the death of the living. For he created all things that they might exist, and the generative forces of the world are wholesome" (1, 13-14).

Israel was to choose between life and death, between the protection of the living God and the ridiculous recourse to the gods of nothingness. This choice is offered to all. What really is the pagans' misfortune is their attachment to idols made by their own hands: "But miserable, with their hopes set on dead things, are the men who gave the name "gods" to the works of men's hands" (13, 10). They confide their life to what is lifeless: "So he takes thought for it, that it may not fall, because he knows that it cannot help itself, for it is only an image and has need of help. When he prays about possessions and his marriage and children, he is not ashamed to address a lifeless thing. For health he appeals to a thing that is weak; for life he prays to a thing that is dead" (13, 16-18).

The diatribe against the worship of idols is pursued with biting irony as christian apologetics will remember.

This is not the first time that the Bible took the idolatry of the pagans to task. Second Isaiah, at the termination of the Exile, severely castigates the cult of false gods: "When you cry out, let your collection of false idols deliver you! The wind will carry them off" (Is. 57, 13).

The invective was not being directed at the pagans, but at the Jews who, succumbing to the contagion, shared their beliefs and adopted their customs.

What is new here is the author of Wisdom uses the same language as did the prophets in order to touch the pagans: "Therefore there will be a visitation also upon the heathen idols, because, though part of what God created, they became an abomination, and became traps for the souls of men and a snare to the feet of the foolish. For the idea of making idols was the beginning of fornication, and the invention of them was the corruption of life, for neither have they existed from the beginning nor will they exist for ever" (14, 11-13).

It is the source of all scandals. We have seen that religious perversion leads to that of all morals: "For the worship of idols not to be named is the beginning and cause and end of every evil. For their worshippers either rave in exultation, or prophesy lies, or live unrightously, or readily commit perjury" (14, 27-18).

And like Israel, when separating themselves from God, the Gentiles hasten to their death: "But just penalties will overtake them on two counts: because they thought wickedly of God in devoting themselves to idols, and because in deceit they swore unrighteously through contempt for holiness" (14, 30).

✿  ✿  ✿

It is possible to snatch oneself from this fatal road. Like the prophets who never despaired of leading Israel back to fidelity even during the most dangerous times, the author of Wisdom does not lose courage in the face of his enormous undertaking. Though the Gentiles are buried in error, God will end up by touching them, overcoming and converting them.

To make himself better understood by the idolatrous people the sage speaks to them in their own language, taking into account the arguments of their wise philosophers, notably the mythographer Evhemer:

"For a father, consumed with grief at an untimely bereavement, made an image of his child, who had been suddenly taken from him; and he now honored as a god what was once a dead human being, and handed on to his dependents secret rites and initiations. Then the ungodly custom, grown strong with time, was kept as a law, and at the command of monarchs graven images were worshipped. When men could not honor monarchs in their presence, since they lived at a distance, they imagined their appearance far away, and made visible images of the king whom they honored, so that by their zeal they might flatter the absent one as though present. Then the ambition of the craftsman impelled even those who did not know the king to intensify their worship. For he, perhaps wishing to please his ruler, skillfully forced the likeness to take a more beautiful form, and the multitude attracted by the charm of his work, now regarded as an object of worship the one whom shortly before they had honored as a man" (14, 15-20).

It is remarkable that the author of Wisdom seeks out the Greeks as his audience by way of preference. Perhaps he feels they are more open to receive the truth.

He reproaches them for not knowing how to go from the creature to the Creator: "For all men who were ignorant of God were foolish by nature; and they were unable from the good things that are seen to know him who exists, nor did they recognize the craftsman while paying heed to his works" (13, 1).

They knew how to discern the reflection of divine beauty in creation. They were so enamored of this that they filled their mind with it and have made it shine out in all their works from east to west. In divinizing the forces of nature they condemned themselves to remaining this side of the truth. The truth they were seeking was what he wanted to impart to them: "Yet these are little to be blamed, for perhaps they go astray while seeking God and desiring to find him. For as they live among his works they keep searching, and they trust in what they see, because the things that are seen are beautiful" (13, 6-7).

The sacred author, visibly moved by this search for beauty, asks himself, not without regret and thus reveals his sympathy for them: "How did they fail to find sooner the Lord of all these things?" (13, 9).

The Jew of Alexandria seems less interested in entering into any dialogue with the natives. Aside from the fact that the task seems very difficult for him, he shares with the Greeks their repugnance for worship offered to animals by the Egyptians. This he never could understand. He expresses his disgust for a religion, the antiquity of which does not suffice to excuse its inhuman character and which cannot even invoke beauty for its justification: "The enemies of thy people worship even the most hateful animals, which are worse than all others, when judged by their lack of intelligence; and even as animals they are not so beautiful in appearance that one would desire them, but they have escaped both the praise of God and his blessing" (15, 18-19).

Though he has a preference for his listeners, he still thinks of the whole pagan world, for all equally stand in need of the truth which is destined for them and will make them free. From whom did God ever turn his face? Although he chose Israel as a testing ground, his solicitude is for the entire humanity. He loves his creature even when the latter forgets him. "For thou lovest all things that exist, and hast loathing for none of the things which thou hast made, for thou wouldst not have made anything if thou hadst hated it" (11, 24).

Has he ever ceased being the God of mercy and justice at whose word spoken on Sinai Moses prostrated himself? "The Lord, a God merciful and gracious, slow to anger, and abounding in steadfast love and faithfulness, keeping steadfast love for thousands, forgiving iniquity and transgression and sin, but who will by no means clear the guilty, visiting the iniquity of the fathers upon the children and the children's children, to the third and fourth generation" (Ex. 34, 6).

His longanimity is not chary of delays as long as the sinner comes to repentance: "But thou art merciful to all, for thou canst do all things, and thou dost overlook men's sins, that they may repent" (11, 23).

It extends to the most hateful of sinners, such as these Canaanites: "Their merciless slaughter of children, and their sacrificial feeding on human flesh and blood. . . . But even these thou didst spare, since they were but men. . . . But judging them little by little thou gavest them a chance to repent, though thou wast not unaware that their origin was evil and their wickedness inborn. . . . For they were an accursed race" (12, 5-11).

Though he punishes the guilty this is not for revenge but instruction. "For the dreams which disturbed them forewarned them of this, so that they might not perish without knowing why they suffered" (18, 19).

The punishment was always in proportion to the fault as the plagues show when they struck the Egyptians: "In return for their foolish and wicked thoughts, which led them astray to worship irrational serpents and worthless animals, thou didst send upon them a multitude of irrational creatures to punish them" (11, 15-16).

This same thing happens to all who live a life of "impiety and folly": "Therefore those who in folly of life lived unrighteously thou didst torment through their own abominations. For they went far astray on the paths of error, accepting as gods those animals which even their enemies despised; they were deceived like foolish babes. Therefore, as to thoughtless children, thou didst send them judgment to mock them" (12, 23-25).

When God punishes, his purpose is to open hearts to repentance that brings about conversion: "Therefore thou dost correct little by little those who trespass, and dost remind and warn them of the things wherein they sin, that they may be freed from wickedness and put their trust in thee, O Lord" (12, 2).

*        *        *

The call to conversion knows neither frontiers nor races. Let us repeat it once more: the Bible has never excluded the rest of the world from its preoccupations; never has it thought Israel should live as though it were alone on earth. Israel is always anxious about the opinion of the Gentiles. Since the Exile, the sacred writers have even paid attention to Yahweh's glory in its radiance over the world. The sacerdotal accounts of Exodus give special evidence of this. God is not content with liberating his people with a strong hand and an outstretched arm: he also intends to make himself known to Pharaoh and his subjects.

The theme of the conversion of nations, however, is met with only in a few isolated texts: "It shall come to pass in the latter days that the mountain of the house of the Lord shall be established as the highest of the mountains, and shall be raised about the hills; and all the nations shall flow to it, and many peoples shall come, and say: 'Come, let us go up to the mountain of the Lord, to the house of the God of Jacob; that he may teach us his ways and that we may walk in his paths" (Is. 2, 2-3; cf. Micah 4, 1-2). "Therefore, behold, I will make them know, this once I will make them know my power and my might, and they shall know that my name is the Lord" (Jer. 16, 21; cf. 12, 15-17). "For when the judgments are in the earth, the inhabitants of the world learn righteousness" (Is. 26, 9; cf. 66, 18).

Although these precious texts which are spread through the text of the prophets' message show the call of God is universal, they were not addressed to the nations themselves. The Book of Wisdom appears to be the first to do this in exhorting them to repentance. It is to the nations, as well as to Israel, that it shows the tragic ruins of Sodom: "Evidence of their wickedness still remains: a continually smoking wasteland, plants bearing fruit that does not ripen, and a pillar of salt standing as a momument to an unbelieving soul" (10, 7).

* * *

What beautiful revenge for the despised Jews to see the repentance of their detractors! Their pride removed, they will have to follow in their footsteps if they do not wish to allow the opportunity of salvation to slip from them; if not, they will forge their own misfortune: "For the wrath of God is revealed from heaven against ungodliness and wickedness of men who by their wickedness suppress the truth" (Rom. 1, 18).

They will justify the judgment of the sages: "For their enemies deserved to be deprived of light and imprisoned in darkness, those who had kept their sons imprisoned, through whom the imperishable light of the law was to be given to the world" (18, 14).

There is no salvation, however, for the nations unless they begin the experience of Israel by accepting it as guide and bearer of the twofold diadem of the Law and Wisdom.

Is this Israel so pure as to merit this following?

So desirous is he to inspire confidence and encourage converts, the author of Wisdom shows a singular silence in dealing with Israel's own weaknesses. While he does not deny them (5, 6-7), they are blurred out in the distant past. When reading his words, one is led to believe that Wisdom has been the possession not of the precious few but of the people as a whole: "Wisdom rescued from troubles those who served her. When a righteous man fled from his brother's wrath, she guided him on the straight paths" (10, 9-10).

Preserving him from sin, "she descended with him into the dungeon, and when he was in prison she did not leave him, until she brought him the scepter of the kingdom" (10, 14).

If, perchance, Israel sinned, its unalterable faith merited for it the right to remain the Elect, the guiding people: " For even if we sin we are thine, knowing thy power; but we will not sin, because we know that we are accounted thine. For to know thee is complete righteousness, and to know thy power is the root of immortality. For neither has the evil intent of human art misled us, nor the fruitless toil of painters, a figure stained with varied colors, whose appearance arouses yearning in fools, so that they desire the lifeless form of a dead image" (15, 2-5).

The reality, as crudely depicted by the prophets, simply gives the lie to this edifying picture of history; and in spite of the sage's effort and the generous thought guiding him, it is difficult not to feel that Israel's testimony was obscured by these pious omissions which reveal a still very imperfect purity. For this testimony to be acceptable, it would have been necessary for Wisdom's author to have acknowledged humbly his people's failures to the same extent as he condemned pagan idolatries.

The Christian, too, has the obligation to denounce errors and vices which give rise to philosophies contrary to Christ's truth. He will never be able to convert those attracted to Buddhism, Islamism, and communism if he imprudently closes his eyes to these evils. He must live his christian faith fully in order to be persuasive. A failure to admit his infidelities and to dissociate them boldly from the ideal he so impatiently wills to share with others deprives the best of causes of any success.

The teaching of the Old Testament, though very lofty, was not able to rise high enough. The Book of Wisdom, in spite of its rare merit, is narrow in its views, taking up once again that opposition between the just and the unjust, and identifying the former with the Jews and the latter with the pagans. And this did not help much in breaking down the barriers between them.

St. Paul, who will take up the case against idolatry in almost the very same words, will give a more realistic picture of the matter. First, it is not for man to judge man: "Therefore you have no excuse, O man, whoever you are, when you judge another" (Rom. 2, 1).

Again, sin is not identified with certain races, with certain beliefs; it is everywhere: "For I have already charged that all men, both Jews and Greeks, are under the power of sin, as it is written: None is righteous, no, not one" (Rom. 3, 10).

Before converting others, convert yourself, or rather open yourself up to conversion by the one who is the source of all grace: "But God, who is rich in mercy, out of the great love with which he loved us, even when we were dead through our trespasses, made us alive together in Christ (by grace you have been saved)" (Eph. 2, 4-5).

To work effectively for the unification of the world, we must remember that no one is as pure as the just one who is perfect and who, leaving his eternity, will soon become man in order to preach, conquer, and save men: "For he is our peace, who has made us both one, and has broken down the dividing wall of hostility, by abolishing in his flesh the law of commandments and ordinances, that he might create in himself one new man in place of the two, so making peace, and might reconcile us both to God in one body through the cross, thereby bringing the hostility to an end" (Eph. 2, 14-16).

It is only in him and through him that his own, in their evangelizing efforts, will aid their unbelieving brothers to discover the light and the truth; for in themselves, their knowledge, talent, wisdom, or even their sanctity would not be sufficient. Each of us manifests and disfigures at one and the same time the face of the Master.

CONCLUSION

# THE OLD TESTAMENT AND
# THE DEVELOPMENT OF THE SPIRITUAL LIFE

Sincerely religious souls understand more and more that a healthy devotion must be founded upon a more exact and profound knowledge of the Scriptures. True piety leads one to draw grace from the perennial spring of the sacraments which support and strengthen it; but the Word of God is also food, a living, rich, strong, and necessary food which prevents spirituality from becoming impoverished and sickly. It is true the Spirit breathes where he wills; but where has one a better opportunity of encountering the Holy Spirit than in the incomparable texts which he himself inspired.

We gladly read then the Gospels, even the Epistles of St. Paul; and this is very good. But the Gospel and everything that can be said of it by the Apostles, the Doctors, and Fathers did not rise up *ex nihilo*, like creation. The Gospel is an ending just as it is a beginning (like the coming of Jesus, his teaching, the drama of Calvary). The Old Testament is not a collection of texts useful for the theologian alone—a mine of teaching offered to the historian, the ethnologist, and the mythologist; a book of stories, poems, proverbs, to be read distractedly by the curious. It is not an anthology spread throughout the liturgy, the most famous parts of which are to be admired by the faithful. But, to be fully profitable, the Old Testament is a reading which is to be done connectedly, meditatively, as such literature merits to be read. And too many Christians, even too many priests, are insufficiently aware of this.

And yet not only would this reading give them a perfect understanding of Jesus, but, in the difficult way of perfection, it would play the role of a guide, the irreplaceable value of which they would quickly recognize.

The spiritual itinerary of the Chosen People—with the difficulties rising up against it and within it, and the help overcoming these difficulties; with the obscurities slowing down its pace and the lights facilitating its march; with the failures of its weakness and the resurgence of its faith; with the closeness of God's Hand leading it towards a goal now seen, now hidden—that spiritual journey of over fifteen hundred years, is the journey of each one of us.

✽ ✽ ✽

The Jews of Christ's time were awaiting a divine intervention which was suddenly to renew all things. Indeed, with the Incarnation, eternity will make a sudden irruption into a humble wintery night; the infinite, into a hidden town of their small country.

But this sudden entrance was prepared patiently and wisely over a long period of time. It has divided history in two. This secret and laborious maturation which our work has attempted to make more comprehensible is described in the parables of the Gospel: the Kingdom of God is comparable to a little pinch of leaven which makes the dough rise; and to the grain of mustard seed which the wind carries away and buries in the ground where it dies and matures and grows into a tree providing shelter for many nests.

What is true of history is nonetheless true of each human existence. The spiritual life obeys laws of growth which regulate every type of life: "I planted, Apollos watered, but God gave growth" (1 Cor. 2, 6). "He who supplies seed to the sower and

bread for food will supply and multiply your resources and increase the harvest of your righteousness" (2 Cor. 9, 10).

There is a part for man to play which must not be stingily calculated or weighed: "So run that you may obtain it" (1 Cor. 9,
24).

Like the runner in the stadium, man must seek perfection with
all his powers. The personal effort is indispensable, for God does
man the honor of undertaking nothing in him without his consent; and it is at the price of a persevering asceticism that the
effort will bring forth fruit: "Therefore, my beloved brethren,
be steadfast, immovable, always abounding in the work of the
Lord, knowing that in the Lord your labor is not in vain" (1 Cor.
15, 58).

But human initiative is not enough: the Stoic or the Yogi is
capable of it. For the Christian, all initiative is already a response
to a call. Man does not grow of himself; to contribute towards
the birth in him of "the perfect man, fully mature with the fullness of Christ himself" (Eph. 4, 13), it would be too little simply
to "cultivate the soul," as Huysmans says, and to have built with
one's own hands the fragile edifice of his virtues: he still needs
what is expressed by St. Paul: "And we all, with unveiled face,
beholding the glory of the Lord, are being changed into his
likeness from one degree of glory to another" (II Cor. 3, 18).

This reflection is not the human virtues shining in his face,
but the high theological virtues, grace, and the deepening in him
of the divine action: ". . . your faith is growing abundantly, and
the love of every one of you for one another is increasing. . . .
This is evidence of the righteous judgment of God, that you may
be worthy of the kingdom of God, for which you are suffering"
(2 Thes. 1, 3-5).

In a word, for the interior man to develop, to fortify, "to be
renewed every day" (2 Cor. 4, 16), he must allow himself to
be formed by the Father in the image of the Son.

Now the entire Old Testament reveals this astonishing transformation effected in us by the divine Hand, retracing in each

of us as it does the phases of the profound life of his People.

A God "of tenderness and pity" fashions it with love; but the material is ungrateful, changeable, or rebellious: Israel is slow to understand, and slower to obey. Then, the divine Potter breaks the defective vase and begins over again and, with a skillful finger, works and reworks it, in order to give it the contour and finish which he had in mind.

The history of Israel, the history of the christian mystery which perpetuates the life, death and resurrection of the Lord, the history of every mystical experience (which is not simply the experience of the supernatural, but of a tutelage both sweet and violent which, by making it pass through the annihilation of Calvary) carries the creature to the glory of infinite Life.

*   *   *

The inspired authors, who tell us this prodigious history, evidently do not give us anything but a fragmentary vision of the greatest of all imaginable dramas: that of the human soul at grips with the Unknowable. Life is too rich to be taken in at a single glance: according to the angle from which one observes it, it reveals only certain aspects of itself. And this is particularly true if there is question of the Spiritual Life.

Though the prophets and sages lead us unfailingly toward the divine Conclusion, it is true that each one follows his own path. It is their work as a whole that permits us to embrace with one look the totality of the divine action. All of us come upon, here and there in their writings, in that great spiritual guidance of a People, our problems, our doubts, our weaknesses; and we can draw from Israel's experience strong and profitable lessons.

The prophets center their attention on the divine exigencies, and they make us conscious of our sinfulness and powerlessness to respond to the Call as long as the Lord himself has not transformed our hearts. The sages make us aware of Wisdom's invitation to take our place at her mystic banquet; it is fitting that we renounce our illusions, that we consent to make the gift of ourselves, that we recognize the true dimensions of our destiny as children of God.

But, before all else, what the prophets and the sages affirm is that this destiny has not glorified the human race except at God's initiative. It is he and he alone who has willed to guide his People since the Exodus from Egypt; and he has not ceased repeating: "I shall be their God and they shall be my people" (Jer. 31, 33).

This Election reveals at first only its advantages: the great Alliance gives rise to springs of water and showers of manna in the most desolate places; a miraculous cloud guides the uncertain march of the tribes; all obstacles, until the Conquest, are swept away. There are the two tablets Moses brought back from the summit of Sinai; but to respect the Decalogue is paying little for the Alliance.

Thus, when God enters our life, what he expects of us appears light when compared to what he gives us: neophytes and converts generally advance in a springtime stupor. The course of existence does not seem changed except that it appears to pass now under a very bright and clear sky: but the Elect scarcely differs from anyone else just as the kingdom of David differed little from the other small States that surrounded it.

The Election, however, is heavy with unforeseeable exigencies. A day comes when God summons us to break with the world around us. He then draws us on to places unknown, through unbroken paths where, amid bushes of thorns, we must cut out a passage. Behind us he has wiped out all our landmarks in order to forestall our cowardliness which is so prompt at making us turn back. This is the divine Adventure which is beginning, in which we must forge ahead and protect ourselves against bogs, as when, in the middle of the eighth century, in the midst of the disordered flock there resounded the rough voice of Amos, the first of the great "troublers" of Israel.

The awakened consciousness quickly perceives the *totalitarian demand* of the divine ownership. In our past life, God was present, but there were also many other masters we were serving unconsciously. And we had easily accommodated ourselves to this syncretism. Henceforth, there must no longer be any "strange gods" in our life, but God alone. And if we are obstinate in sharing the integral love he expects from us, he reproaches us through the mouth of HOSEA for having prostituted ourselves as did Israel.

To regain our equilibrium we are then tempted like Juda at the time of ISAIAH to lean upon the resources of our intelligence and will, on the help of men, on all these weak powers. And now there is no other support but God for our frailty. To convince us of this he abandons us to ourselves: without understanding it immediately, we multiply our efforts as does the man in quicksand who panics: and we only bury ourselves deeper and deeper in our misery. Then, we must renounce all desire of saving ourselves; it is better to call upon the help of the One who can draw us out of danger. Faith, purified of its human dross, gives us back the hope of life: "Emmanuel! God with us!"

But, though our anguish has given rise to this confidence and to this fidelity, it is still difficult to advance along the naked terrain where the powerful Hand is leading us, and quickly we experience its firmness rather than its gentleness: the former is perceptible now, the latter reveals itself only at a distance. And then there are the weaknesses, the discouragements, and perhaps even doubts. We were good, or at least we believed we were; but these stumbling blocks, these failures, and these incessant falls are disconcerting. Did we really have so many secret or unavowed attachments? Was our march so pitiably barred by our human heaviness? Were we so enslaved? Who were we then? We must really admit it: we are nothing but sinners;

and this is what makes up our misery. And we shall discover that what is needed, to deliver us from ourselves, is a *new heart,* about which JEREMIAH speaks, on which the Law will be written which we still look upon as exterior to ourselves.

This type of heart alone which God will place in us is capable of answering, with the spontaneous freshness of the "Ecce," and the "Fiat," the call of God. This heart alone will reveal the true meaning of this New Man, of whom we have so frequently heard: "Do not lie to one another, seeing that you have put off the old nature with its practices and have put on the new nature, which is being renewed in knowledge after the image of its creator" (Col. 3, 9-10). This heart alone will make this teaching a reality of our life.

This new life, however, has death as a condition; and this death must be accepted: is it not to trace out the way for us that Christ has placed the Cross of Golgotha as a stepping stone to the Resurrection? The death of the "old man" will realize this *purity* in us about which EZEKIEL was obsessed.

Then, in our certainty that the Word of God alone remains, that his Hand extended over the universe has really incorporated us into the Kingdom of the New Covenant, we shall sing, with the SECOND ISAIAH, the perfect hymn of thanksgiving and love, as children who have really understood what the name *Father* implies: "Bring my sons from afar and my daughters from the end of the earth, every one who is called by my name, whom I created for my glory, whom I formed and made" (Is. 43, 6-7). "And I will be father to you, and you shall be my sons and daughters, says the Lord Almighty" (1 Cor. 6, 18).

Thus, from Amos to the great unknown prophet of the Exile, we run along a road that leads us to the heart of the mystery of our baptism.

This spiritual evolution moreover, which makes us discover through a personal and lived experience the grace of the divine ownership and its inestimable price along with its rigorous conditions, is not a single event that takes place in our life. The formation of Israel was a work which was interrupted and begun over and over again.

Each one of us in proportion to his age, knows this very well: our formation is renewed at times with the regularity of a liturgical cycle. Is it without reason that the Church punctuates our life by the annual recalling of the Passion and the Resurrection of the Lord?

The spiritual work is always beginning again without our knowing exactly where we are in it. *"Our soul is like a sealed letter which God alone is able to read,"* says St. John of the Cross. The Day of the Lord never comes here below.

In any case, our repeated conversions, at whatever level or standard they may be, present the same process: there is the call, the joy of the promises, the discovery of the exigencies, the admission to our weakness, the consciousness of our sinful condition, and the abandonment into the Hands of the Father. Although our mediocrity too often makes a wearisome "reiteration" of these conversions, where we allow ourselves to be raised by merciful grace only to fall again into the depths of our misery, yet more faithful souls, whose flight is acquainted with irregularities, resume their spiritual ascent with increased altitude each time, as is done by certain birds.

Should we not compare these repeated flights, that send them higher into the light of the heights, to the gradual advance which brought Israel from its still rough fidelity which Amos stirred up to the humble and fervent surrender, sustained by the prophets of the Exile, of that "small remnant" from which will spring the new People?

❖   ❖   ❖

The sages, taking the place of the prophets, tell us in advance about our spiritual itinerary.

The divine Call, a warm call filled with promises, resounds in the depths of our hearts: this is what the Introduction to the Book of PROVERBS tells us.

Too many superficial minds, either from ignorance or from fear of "contagion," believe they can explain the spiritual élan of the "Called" by some deception of some secret grief which, giving them a disgust of the world, makes them leave the world. However, neither resentment, neither discouragement, nor revolt is able to sustain the person in the Quest for God. One does not enter upon spiritual paths with an exact and authentic Call which generates happiness, enthusiasm, love, and the desire of the Absolute.

On the contrary, it is true that Wisdom compels her follower to *choose*, then to renounce and break with, as Abram had to leave the opulence of Chaldea in order to bury himself in the unknown paths of the Desert; just as the Apostles will leave all to follow Jesus. But, in exchange for this renunciation, Wisdom makes us enter a new world which is above and before even creation itself, where we feel ourselves freed from the heaviness which nailed us to the earth.

A generous leaven was rising in souls; but then comes dryness. Every human enterprise knows this disenchantment, and the novice's ardor soon cools off within the bare walls of his cell. The road along which the Elect advances is sure; but the glimpsed goal is blurred out: the clouds have hidden the horizon, and it is towards the unknown that he walks sustained alone by *faith*. As one writer puts it: "Did you imagine it as a beautiful avenue opening out upon a level and sanded park? Rather, it is a dangerous path, rough and unadorned, on the side of a mountain and in a hewn rock."

The forward thrust has now given way to a certain giddiness; hope, to shock. With Job, we sigh: "Where are you leading us, Lord?" Bitterly we confront, like the holy man, our actual misery and the tranquillity we were enjoying before having felt the weight of God's Hand. Everything then seemed possible, and now we see ourselves in total destitution; we amounted to something before, and now we are no longer anything.

This is a gross temptation, some will say, which takes hold only of less noble souls. The experience is necessary: no less than Job, St. Thérèse of the Child Jesus experienced it in her Carmel. Illusory and sterile was the tranquillity of former times; fruitful, today's destitution. And the theophany which concludes the drama of Job renews him in his vocation, imposing upon him the necessity of continuing his route without seeking to understand where God is leading him.

If we do not understand, it is because we are able to cast only a human glance over everything: what is a set-back? what is success? Is it reasonable, or even licit, to expect anything whatsoever *under the sun?* To afflict oneself about what is, to dream about what is not, to long after the impossible, all this, says QOHELETH, is equally vain. Wisdom is to accept what God is giving at the present moment, the best and the worst, with gratitude or resignation; to work without illusion as well as without indolence: to give up the desire of piercing through the mystery of our destiny.

But, the more one progresses along the way of the mystical life, the more one must arm himself with *good sense.* Is he to lose his head at night? The Elect has nothing about him of the "tragic hero" who acts out his sad despair in romantic dramas. The spiritual history of a man is not made up of catastrophes and deceptions, which provoke the passionate cries of a Job or the bitter sarcasms of a Qoheleth. Trials are not a permanent state, but accidents, more or less frequent or prolonged, the usefulness of which ends sooner or later proving itself. But, side by side with these trials and in these trials themselves, the soul that wishes to give herself to God finds the most invigorating of foods in a sane Wisdom, conscious of her resources, well ordered, as that which BEN SIRA teaches. The soul will acquire for the vicissitudes ahead a balance which far from obstructing the divine action will facilitate it.

When there will arise, in fact, the great tribulations which, as at the time of Antiochus, will demand fearless heroism and total sacrifice, the Christian formed by this robust and enlightened Wisdom will face them with nothing but firmness. If we add to this the bravery of DANIEL, founded upon the certitude that in every circumstance the faithful soul is in the Hands of God, the Christian will brave even death: "And not one of them (sparrows) will fall to the ground without your Father's will" (Matt. 10, 29).

To fortify the persecuted Jews, whose spirituality, besides, had done without the perspective of a heaven or a hell during a period of a millennium, the Lord had opened for them the "Sealed Book," in which was inscribed the eschatological triumph of the saints over time and history.

The Christian, from the beginning, has this advantage over Israel of not being ignorant of the reality of the retribution which awaits him after death. But is it not at the crucial hours that it will be good for him to remember this more, to make of it less a speculation for his mind and more a food for his heart? Assiduous meditation on the *last ends*, as long as it is not "lived," runs the risk, it seems to us, of being nothing but an artificial exercise: there are certain values which never should be spoiled. This meditation, besides, places the accent on man when it should first be placed on God; on an imperfect view of eternity, which does not begin after death, but in which we are living from the moment grace touched us. And yet, for all that, this same meditation regains a singular virtue when it becomes vital for us and when it imposes upon us, as upon the Jews of the second century, the choice between sacrifice *"usque ad mortem"* and the evasions of human prudence.

*Bearers of God,* finally, we shall know contradiction, hatred, and contempt (Matt. 24, 9ff.). But, no more than does WISDOM, we shall not respond by bad temper, resentment, or the morbid thirst of personal revenge. We must not avenge ourselves on anyone, but we must give testimony before all of the Law of truth and love which generations, after having received it from the Apostles, so faithfully transmitted. In our condition, as humble and humiliated as it may be, we possess as a treasure a faith filled with infinity; and we are vested with a grandeur which, though it escapes fleshly eyes, is real. This grandeur, made out of our own littleness and God's power, we must share with others and have a consuming desire to do so.

In order that others may accept the invitation of running in the path of this marvelous Adventure, of finding the itinerary traced out by the prophets and the sages and offered to anyone who desires to come after the Master, it is necessary that we ourselves know how to bury our life in that of Christ, to be for them worthwhile examples. We shall not make them do this, unless we do it ourselves: "For you have died, and your life is hid with Christ in God. When Christ who is our life appears, then you will appear with him in glory" (Col. 3, 3-4).

On this condition and in proportion as we shall allow the Lord to act through us, the work of universal conversion, which was in Wisdom only a presentiment, will continue to be realized.

In conclusion, such is the great lesson we shall retain from our reading of the prophets and the sages which we shall not cease to meditate upon: if the former, bringing to light our powerlessness before the divine demands, open the perspective of regenerating grace, and if the latter empty us of our illusions, to give place to God's action, both the one and the other teach us to lose ourselves under the Hand of God, to rise up from it as New Men: "Humble yourselves therefore under the mighty hand of God, that in due time he may exalt you" (1 Pet. 5, 6).

❂    ❂    ❂

## Persian Period

| | | |
|---|---|---|
| 539 | Babylon falls to Cyrus | |
| 522 | Darius I | |
| 500 | First tragedies of Aeschylus | Introduction to the |
| 490 | Marathon | book of Proverbs |
| 486 | Xerxes I | |
| 480 | Salamis | |
| | | |
| 465 | Artaxerxes I. Pericles of Athens | Job |
| 442 | Antigone of Sophocles | |
| | | |
| 343 | Aristotle of Alexandria | Ecclesiastes |
| 334 | Alexander | (Qoheleth) |

## Greco-Roman Period

| | | |
|---|---|---|
| 323 | Ptolemies in Egypt. Palestine under their domination | Cycle of the Daniel stories |
| | | |
| 223 | Antiochus III, (the Great) of Antioch (Seleucids). Simon II, high priest of Jerusalem | |
| | | |
| 198 | Victory of Panion over Egypt — Jerusalem falls to Seleucids | Ecclesiasticus |
| | | |
| 188 | Victory of Romans at Magnesia | |
| 175 | Antiochus IV Epiphanes | |
| 171 | Onias III, high priest dies at Antioch | |
| | | |
| 167 | The great persecution. Maccabean Revolt | Book of Daniel |
| 164 | Antiochus IV died | |
| | | |
| 134 | John Hyrcanus and the Hasmoneans | |
| | | |
| 117 | Ptolemy VIII, persecutor of Jews in Egypt | |
| 63 | Pompey takes Jerusalem | Wisdom |
| 30 | Egypt becomes a Province of Rome | |
| 20 | Birth of Philo of Alexandria | |